Chapters
of
Steam

Chapters Of Steam

John Sagar M.A., Ph.D.

Map and line drawings by John W. Holroyd

October 1984

ISBN 0 946184 11 9

Designed by Roger Hardingham
Published by
Kingfisher Railway Productions
22 Ripstone Gardens, Highfield, Southampton, SO2 3RE

This book is dedicated to the Locomotive Department of the Worth Valley Railway.

Raw material for a Worth Valley restoration crew. No. 75078 at Barry scrapyard in 1972. It is interesting to compare this photograph with those on pages 123-129.

Howard Malham

Frontispiece: Classic Worth Valley steam, as a vintage locomotive does battle with the severe Yorkshire gradients. No. 52044 approaches Damems loop on 22nd March 1975.

John Sagar

Contents

Introduction

Since its closure by British Railways in 1962, the Worth Valley Railway has acquired, or played host to, a range of steam locomotives without parallel in Britain. Few indeed can have been the members of the embryonic Keighley and Worth Valley Railway Preservation Society who, in the early 1960s, envisaged that one day services on this now famous branch line would be worked turn and turn about by a former regular engine on the celebrated 'Golden Arrow' Pullman train and an American-built 2-8-0 purchased from behind the Iron Curtain: that such revered steam locomotives as **Flying Scotsman, Evening Star** and even **Lion** would ever traverse Worth Valley metals: or that Haworth would eventually aspire to the heights of a main line servicing depot, preparing locomotives to work charter trains over the nationalised network.

Great things have been achieved since those early days. Since 1965 more than fifty steam locomotives have, at some time or other, been resident on the Worth Valley Railway. More than forty of these have made public appearances in steam. This is a remarkably high percentage when one considers the tribulations inherent in steam preservation. Since we are fast approaching the twentieth anniversary of the first arrival of rolling stock at Haworth under Preservation Society auspices, this moment seems opportune to pay tribute to the multi-faceted character of the Railway's motive power and the unpaid, unsparing efforts of all the volunteers who have presented us with such a dazzling mobile feast. The present album addresses itself to this not inconsiderable task.

My aims in selecting the illustrations for **'Chapters of Steam'** have been essentially twofold. First, to provide some tangible record of the multifarious careers of all these engines, illustrate which duties they performed prior to retirement and show how, almost miraculously, many scenes from their past have survived into preservation. Second, to chart how the Worth Valley Railway itself has evolved under private ownership. It is becoming increasingly modish in railway publishing circles for

The start of it all. A work-stained 'B1' 4-6-0 No. 61161 hauls Barton Wright 'Ironclad' 0-6-0 No. 957 and Gresley 'N2/2' 0-6-2T No. 69523 past Shipley Guiseley Junction, en route to Keighley, on 26th February 1965. Also included in the consignment is a former Manchester, Sheffield & Lincolnshire Railway four-wheeled carriage of 1876 vintage. By this date, 'Pug' 0-4-0ST No. 51218 and Manning, Wardle 0-6-0ST **Sir Berkeley** had already been delivered to Haworth. Nos. 957 and 69523 were drawn up the Worth Valley to their new home on 6th March 1965 by Captain W.G. Smith's Great Northern Railway 'J52' 0-6-0ST No. 1247. The Ilkley line can be seen diverging at the left of the picture, whilst the embankment above the train carries the now-closed G.N.R. route to Idle.

Robin Lush

No. 8431 outside Haworth new locomotive shed, May 1984.   **John Sagar**

photographs depicting bustling activity to be juxtaposed with more recent views of despoliation and irrevocably altered landscapes. On the Worth Valley, as on other preserved railways, this process is thankfully very much reversed. Weed-strewn tracks, dilapidated buildings and pathetic, rusting locomotive hulks have reverted to their original role as integral parts of a successful, cared-for railway. Indeed, so great is the contrast to the early days of the Preservation Society that the founding fathers might have been forgiven had they had second thoughts and contented themselves with gardening, or some such less taxing pursuit!

Assembling the photographs for publication has been an immensely enjoyable, rewarding if at times slightly frustrating task. It is a sad but inescapable irony that general improvements in photographic technique and inventiveness, and the availability of quality equipment at reasonable prices, coincided very much with the demise of steam on B.R. and its disappearance from most industrial locations. One also rapidly learns that railway photographers were more active in some parts of the country than in others and that glamorous express locomotives appealed more to their cameras than did humble shunters. Even with steam engines, it appears, familiarity can breed contempt! Whereas the Worth Valley's locomotives are now captured on film many thousands of times each year, this was most certainly not the case before they came to Haworth. I have nevertheless done everything possible to provide a representative selection of pictures and crave the indulgence of any readers who feel that their favourites have received a raw deal.

Sharp-eyed individuals will doubtless be quick to point out that this album includes certain Worth Valley-based locomotives which have now moved on and distinguished themselves in other fields. This has been done because it was felt important to portray all those steam engines which have made an impact on the Worth Valley scene over the past twenty years. For this reason I have also omitted altogether engines such as **Harlaxton, Isabel, BEA No. 2** and **Ackton Hall No. 3**.

The story does not, of course, end here. It requires great resources of human endeavour and finance to keep the Worth Valley's fleet operational. If this book encourages people to come and join in this task, and sample the warm Yorkshire welcome which undoubtedly awaits them at Haworth, it will have been a most worthwhile undertaking. Furthermore, the Worth Valley Railway has recently embarked on a new engine shed and workshop complex at Haworth which, when complete, will put it in the very forefront of steam locomotive maintenance centres. So as to ensure that there will be adequate material for a second volume of **Chapters of Steam** in another twenty years, all proceeds from this volume are earmarked for this worthy project.

Finally, and most importantly, I should like to thank the many friends and fellow-photographers who have given so freely of their time and enthusiasm to see this project through to fruition. My particular thanks go to Richard Greenwood and Robin Higgins for their attention to historical and mechanical detail and their forthright views on what constitutes a good picture! Any defects in the book should be ascribed to me alone.

JOHN SAGAR
Bury, July 1984

Map of the
Worth Valley Railway

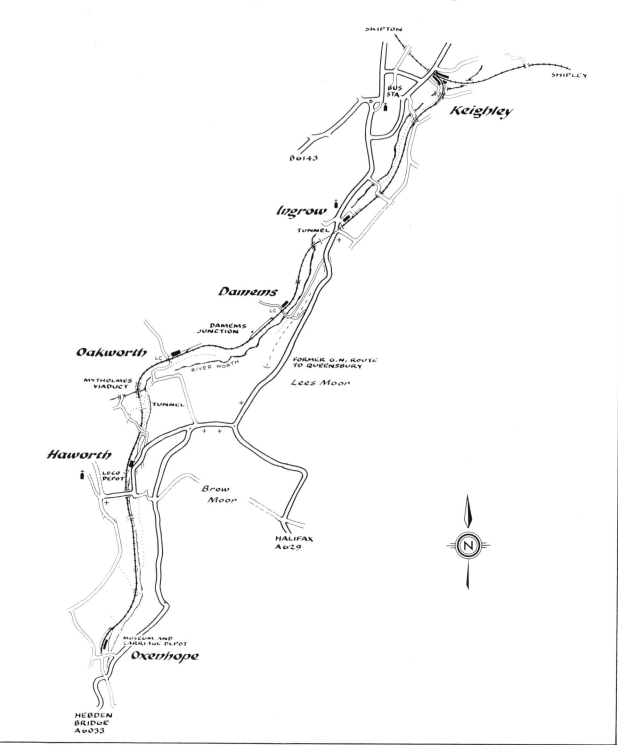

LANCASHIRE & YORKSHIRE RAILWAY 0-4-0 SADDLE TANKS Nos. 19 and 51218

No fewer than fifty-seven of these tiny locomotives were built between 1891 and 1910 and the two survivors are to be found on the Worth Valley Railway. Designed by J.A.F. Aspinall and closely modelled on three 0-4-0 saddle tanks supplied to the L. & Y.R. by Vulcan Foundry in 1886, the 'Pugs', as they quickly became known, were initially built to shunt the dock lines at Fleetwood, Goole and Liverpool. No. 51218 holds a special place in Worth Valley affections, having been the first item of stock to arrive in 1965. It was in frequent use in the early years of the Preservation Society.

Nos. 19 and 2, both built in 1910, stand at Newton Heath shed on 26th June 1926, still carrying their L. & Y.R. livery. Both engines were withdrawn from L.M.S. service in 1931, No. 2 going for scrap in July of that year and No. 19 being sold to the contractor John Mowlem the following September. No. 19 boasts a spark arrester for working in warehouses and both 'Pugs' have their whistle in the original position on the cab roof. A fatal accident at Preston about 1930 resulted in this fitting being moved to the cab front. The Newton Heath 'Pugs' shunted the potato yard at Oldham Road Low Level goods depot and further merited their nickname of 'potato engines' because of their capacity to produce delicious roast potatoes under their dome covers! By coincidence, the pits in the new locomotive shed at Haworth were constructed by Mowlems in 1983.

H.C. Casserley

Having moved on in 1935 to the Charlton, London, works of United Glass Bottle Manufacturers Ltd., No. 19 was named **Prince**. In this 1949 view, the locomotive has acquired a non-standard whistle, a new smokebox door and a different lubrication system. Its injector overflow has been re-routed, the trailing sandbox modified and the slidebar cover has disappeared. By the early 1960s **Prince** was running in maroon livery.

Frank Jones

No. 19 was initially purchased privately for preservation and spent some time at the Luton depot of the London Railway Preservation Society. Whilst at this location it was given a hasty repaint in L.M.S. livery. Ownership subsequently passed to the L. & Y.R. Saddletanks Fund and the engine is seen shortly after arrival at Haworth in November 1967.

Howard Malham

The need for extensive and costly repairs has unfortunately meant that No. 19's career on the Worth Valley has been spent as a static exhibit at Oxenhope Museum. It now carries the L. & Y.R. goods engine livery of black with red lining and number plates of the correct pattern have re-appeared on the cab sides.

John Sagar

The earliest known shot of No. 68 (alias No. 51218), thought to have been taken at Agecroft in pre-grouping days. Worthy of attention are the re-railing jack and the early rear sandbox which was filled through a flap. With this arrangement the box tended to fill with water. Later the flap was replaced by a spout and cap.

Eric Mason

No. 11218 at an unknown location during the Stanier era on the L.M.S. The whistle remains in the early position and the trailing sandbox is still unmodified. In common with several other 'Pugs', No. 11218 was not accorded a smokebox number plate in L.M.S. days.
Richard S. Greenwood collection

With the passing years the 'Pugs' wandered far beyond the original L. & Y.R. system, their diminutive proportions making them highly suitable for operation on sharply curved track and in confined areas. A long way from home, Nos. 51218 and 51217 stand at Barrow Road shed, Bristol, on 28th May 1961. Wearing the trilby hat is the late Harold Morris, Shedmaster at Bath Green Park from 1956 until the closure of the Somerset and Dorset in 1966. At his side is the late Norman Lockett, a very fine railway photographer for over sixty years.
Ivo Peters

No. 51218 saw frequent service at Haworth in the early days of the Preservation Society, as in this Spring 1966 picture of it shunting the weed-covered yard. The former Metropolitan Railway carriages behind the engine are in the initial Worth Valley livery of blue and primrose. This was ultimately discarded because of difficulties in keeping it clean in the harsh Yorkshire climate. With the construction of the new engine shed this scene has now changed beyond recognition.

John Sagar

In February 1967 No. 51218 temporarily left Haworth. It was booked to work three brake van trips on the 19th of that month over the steeply-graded line from Rochdale to Whitworth, closed to passengers since 1947. The weather varied from brilliant sunshine to violent hailstorms and the crowds of lineside spectators provided a foretaste of the drawing power of modern-day B.R. steam specials. No. 51218 acquitted itself well in the circumstances and is here depicted on Entwisle Road viaduct, between Rochdale and Wardleworth, with the final trip of the day.

Martin Welch

Dwarfed by Stanier locomotives, No. 51218 makes an incongruous spectacle at Trafford Park shed on 20th May 1967. Already a preserved engine, the 'Pug' had just completed the first of two periods on loan to Messrs. Brown and Polson of Trafford Park as stand-in for their ailing Barclay. The following day it worked a rail tour round the Trafford Park Estate lines.

Richard S. Greenwood

Back on Worth Valley metals, No. 51218 struggles manfully from Haworth to Oxenhope with a L. & Y.R. Saddletanks Fund AGM special on 5th January 1975. No. 51218 was the first engine acquired by the Fund, being purchased in 1964 on withdrawal from B.R. service at Neath depot in Glamorgan.

John Sagar

No. 51218 takes a curtain call during the Shildon cavalcade to celebrate the 150th anniversary of the Stockton & Darlington Railway, 31st August 1975. Weighing a mere 21 tons 5 cwt in working order, No. 51218 was the second smallest engine in the cavalcade and made an impact far beyond its size! The journey to and from Shildon was made by low-loader lorry. The vacuum train pipe fitted since preservation can be clearly seen looping round the trailing sandbox. Note also the bell on the cab front. Most 'Pugs' had bells, but the normal position was between the frames.

Ben Wade

The 'Pug' marks its 75th birthday by hauling the L. & Y.R. saloon of 1878 up the Worth Valley on 31st October 1976. It is seen crossing Bridge 27, which was in the course of rebuilding.

Martin Welch

15

MANCHESTER SHIP CANAL RAILWAY 0-6-0 SIDE TANKS Nos. 31 'HAMBURG' and 67

The Manchester Ship Canal Railway was the largest independent industrial railway in the country, with over seventy engines to its credit. Most common locomotives were the Hudswell, Clarke 0-6-0Ts in both short and long side tank versions. Still largely in 'as built' condition, No. 31 rests outside the sub-shed at No. 9 Dock in June 1955.

Frank Jones

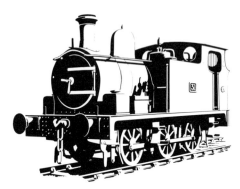

During its first winter of operation, 1968-69, the Worth Valley Railway ran an all-line basic steam service at weekends. No. 31 was a stalwart performer on this service and certainly looked the part when fitted with a cut-down snowplough from an '8F' 2-8-0. In this form the engine makes a spirited departure from Keighley with its two-coach train on a crisp day.

John S. Whiteley

Latterly, No. 31's activities have been restricted to the mid-winter shuttle service between Haworth and Oxenhope and bursts of activity on Enthusiasts' Weekends. Indeed, so prodigious is the locomotive's pulling capacity that it has gained the nickname 'Mighty Mouse'. More officially, No. 31's original name **Hamburg**, removed after angry demonstrations by Salford dockers on the eve of the Great War, was restored to the locomotive on 17th March 1972. **Hamburg** is also now adorned in a pseudo-German livery, with red wheels and coupling rods. In this guise, No. 31 clambers up to Ingrow on April Fool's Day, 1979. The new taller chimney, fitted in the mid-1970s, merely adds to the 'olde worlde' appearance.

John Sagar

Right: Works train duty also frequently came No. 31's way after its arrival at Haworth. On 8th August 1971 it was given the task of working a train of B.R. wagons of ballast up the branch, at passenger train speed, in connection with shed construction at Oxenhope. The mission was accomplished and No. 31 is seen at the line's southern terminus, where the platform had still to be surfaced and the improvised water tower continued in use.

Robin Higgins

Left: No. 31's snowplough was really fitted for filming purposes, and not to allay apprehension about Worth Valley winters! Somewhat remarkably, No. 31 had been chosen to masquerade as a Russian locomotive for the BBC2 version of Tolstoy's 'Resurrection' during the Autumn of 1968. With numerous dummy fittings and a suitably decrepit collection of vehicles to pull, No. 31 is captured at Ingrow during a lull in filming.

Keith Preston

No. 67, the Worth Valley's second former Ship Canal engine, has extended water tanks which enable it to carry 260 gallons more than No. 31. In outline, it is distinctly reminiscent of the L.N.E.R. 'J50' class tank engines, once a common sight in West Yorkshire. In this picture, taken at Mode Wheel on the MSC system, No. 67 still sports the green livery, lined out in yellow, which was later superseded by black. The locomotive has split brasses on the side rods and the Ramsbottom safety valves have not yet been supplanted by the Ross Pop variety.

Frank Jones

Right: By 1957, No. 67 was painted black and had been given solid eye bushes on the side rods. Note also the Ross Pop safety valves.

Frank Jones

Opposite page: After being purchased for preservation by Dr. J.G. Blears, No. 67 was used for several trips over the Ship Canal system and Trafford Park Estate lines. It was also given a Hunslet dome (squarer than the original) and in this form is seen crossing Westinghouse Road, Stretford with a Roch Valley Railway Society special on 29th October 1967.

Peter Eastham

Left: No. 67 has not seen active service on the Worth Valley for several years. Before it was withdrawn for extensive overhaul, the long-tank Hudswell, Clarke leaves Oxenhope for Haworth on a Summer shuttle train on 28th August 1970. Unusually for the Worth Valley, the engine is pointing chimney-first downhill. The former North Eastern Railway slotted-post signal was erected in 1968 for the BBC t.v. version of 'The Railway Children' and will eventually feature in Oxenhope Museum.

John Sagar

TAFF VALE RAILWAY 0-6-2 SIDE TANK No. 52

Built by Neilson Reid of Glasgow in 1899 as Taff Vale Railway No. 85, the first member of that Railway's '02' class of 0-6-2T, this engine was brought to the Worth Valley in January 1971. After the absorption of the Taff Vale by the Great Western Railway, it was discarded as surplus to requirements in the G.W.R.'s drive for locomotive standardisation. Purchased in 1929 by the Lambton, Hetton & Joicey Colliery Company in Co. Durham, No. 52 was used successfully for many years on coal trains from collieries to the coast.

Below: Of particular interest in this picture of No. 52 in L.H. & J.C. days are the brass number plates and safety valve cover, the dumb buffers for shunting narrow gauge wagons and the smokebox wing plates.

Frank Jones

A delightfully evocative view of No. 52 by the coaling stage at Philadelphia on 13th June 1967. Note the large smokebox door and modified hand rail.

Ivo Peters

Right: No. 52 as restored to L.H. & J.C. green livery and displayed at Oxenhope.

John Sagar

Left: Following nationalisation of the coal industry in 1947, No. 52 continued hard at work from the Philadelphia depot at Houghton-le-Spring until finally displaced by diesels in 1968. In somewhat dilapidated condition, No. 52 heads a rake of loaded coal wagons at Philadelphia on 29th June 1965. By this date a modified, cut-down cab and bunker had been fitted and the brass fittings and dumb buffers of earlier years had been removed.

Howard Malham

STEWARTS & LLOYDS 0-6-0 SADDLE TANKS Nos. 57 'SAMSON', 62 and 63 'CORBY'

During post-war expansion of their Northamptonshire ironstone system, the celebrated steel manufacturing company of Stewarts & Lloyds ordered nine large saddle tank locomotives from Robert Stephenson and Hawthorn of Newcastle-on-Tyne. The first seven, Nos. 56-62, appeared in 1950, to be followed by No. 63 in 1954 and No. 64 as late as 1958. Allocated to Pen Green depot, they served the extensive quarries and ironstone mines near Corby until replaced by diesels in the late 1960s.

On 11th May 1964, No. 63 keeps company with the smaller and considerably more handsome 0-6-0ST No. 34 **Calettwr** on the S. & L. system.

Ivo Peters

No. 57 at the end of a hard day's work in 1964. The sheer bulk of these engines cannot fail to impress, but the truncated saddle tank is not an aesthetic triumph.

Frank Jones

No fewer than three of these imposing locomotives were purchased by Worth Valley members and all came to Haworth in the Spring of 1969. The first to arrive was No. 63, which was promptly repainted blue, fitted with vacuum brake and placed in regular passenger service. She quickly showed that she and her sisters would be capable of hauling heavy passenger trains, but the level of comfort for the crew was not to everyone's taste. In August 1969, No. 63 stands at Keighley, where the weed-choked platform 3 is still in use for B.R. parcels traffic.

Howard Malham

No. 62 in bucolic setting. In B.R.-style dark green livery and with Worth Valley crest on its tank, this chunky machine essays a 'toy train' image at Mytholmes, 9th March 1975.

John Sagar

After a long period under repair following its initial stint of Worth Valley service, No. 63 reappeared in a somewhat smarter blue livery and received the name **Corby** in recognition of its association with that town. On 8th April 1984 it shunts a motley rake of stock at Haworth comprising a G.W.R. brake van and L.M.S. and L.N.E.R. parcels vans.

John Sagar

Left:

No. 57 has been aptly named **Samson** on the Worth Valley and painted red. In typically aggressive mood, the engine crosses the River Worth near Ingrow on Silver Jubilee Day, 7th June 1977, with the 17.02 from Keighley.

John Sagar

In May 1982, No. 62 was transferred to the Bury base of the East Lancashire Railway Preservation Society. It has since visited the North Yorkshire Moors Railway and looks very much in control as it barks away from Levisham with a Pickering train, 29th April 1984. A further move in July 1984 took this engine to Isfield in East Sussex.

John Sagar

SOUTHERN RAILWAY 'USA' CLASS 0-6-0 SIDE TANK No. 72

With its striking light brown livery, an intriguing amalgam of Milwaukee Road 'Hiawatha' practice and Stroudley's 'improved engine green' of the London, Brighton & South Coast Railway, No. 72 is a familiar, not to say controversial part of the Worth Valley scene. One of fourteen such locomotives bought by the Southern Railway from the United States Army Transportation Corps in 1946 for use at Southampton Docks, No. 72 was built by the Vulcan Ironworks, Wilkes-Barre, Pennsylvania in 1943 and subsequently shipped to Britain. As far as is known, No. 72 was little used here during the war, though it did venture across the Channel after D-Day and worked for a short period at Arromanches locomotive depot. It was finally withdrawn from B.R. service in 1967, having gained a certain amount of celebrity as Guildford shed pilot. The following year it shared with No. 41241 the honour of hauling the reopening train on the Worth Valley Railway. Since then, its resounding chime whistle, distinctive silver smokebox and tendency to emit heavy exhausts – still not totally eliminated despite conversion to oil firing – have brought a welcome 'Yankee' flavour to the Railway.

Shortly before nationalisation, No. 72 stands at Southampton Docks on 21st September 1947 with a sister locomotive and L. & S.W.R. 'B4' 0-4-0 tanks for company. Original features still on the locomotive are the bunker, round cab windows (front and rear), injectors and clacks, American whistle and handle at the front of the side tank. In addition to those examples purchased by the Southern Railway, 'USA' tanks even gravitated as far as the Manchester Ship Canal and Mersey Docks & Harbour Board systems for a time. Bank Hall shed actually contemplated using them to replace their L. & Y.R. 'Pugs'.

H.C. Casserley

Above: 1964 'USA' quartet at Eastleigh, comprising Nos. 30072, 30073, 30071 and 30069. Note No. 30073 in lined green livery. Unfortunately, only No. 30072 survives.

R.J. Buckley

The 'USA' tanks were popular performers on rail tours and this provided a welcome escape from their normal menial duties. On the misty morning of 9th October 1966, No. 30072 passes Dundonald Road level crossing, Wimbledon, with the Southern Counties Touring Society's 'Four Counties Special' train.

Eric Knight

The desolation that was Salisbury, Summer 1967, as locomotives with many useful years' service left in them sadly await their fate. Fortunately No. 30064, the locomotive seen parked in front of No. 30072, was also saved and can now be found on the Bluebell Railway in Sussex.

Worthrail Photo Archive

No. 30072 first saw Worth Valley service as works train engine on a bitterly cold 24th February 1968. The hose looped round the dome had been placed there in an attempt to thaw it out, and should not be interpreted as a primitive example of Worth Valley locomotive plumbing! Coaching stock is the ex-Southern Railway 3rd class brake No. 3554 and G.N.R. Bogie Milk Van No. M4151 (scrapped in 1971). The drab black livery of No. 30072 as delivered was doubtless instrumental in its later colourful transformation.

Howard Malham

Prior to the granting of the Light Railway Order, the Worth Valley branch was inspected by Colonel J.H. Robertson on 8th June 1968. At the end of a successful day, No. 72 passes Oakworth, en route to Haworth, with the empty stock of the inspection train.

Ken Roberts

Another picture of No. 72 on 8th June 1968. At the time, it carried a chime whistle from a B.R. 'Britannia' Pacific. The grim tenements by Keighley bank were clearly ripe for demolition!

John Fozard

The reopening special at Oxenhope, awaiting return to Keighley, 29th June 1968. The overgrown yard has since been transformed by the erection of exhibition and carriage maintenance sheds and servicing platforms.

John S. Whiteley

On 1st July 1976 the Worth Valley Railway pre-empted American Bicentennial celebrations by running its own 'Bicentennial Special'. No. 72 was temporarily renumbered 1776 and the cab sides were emblazoned with the original version of the stars and stripes. By now, No. 72 had been converted to oil firing and had received a new bunker. Note also the generator and bell in front of the chimney, the 'A4' whistle and the smokebox number plate. The run-round facilities via platform 3 at Keighley were still something of a novelty, having only come into use the previous April.

John Sagar

Right: Saturday 24th June 1978 saw No. 72 aptly heading a tenth anniversary special train in Ebor Lane cutting. Unfortunately No. 41241 was out of service.

John Sagar

Below: Nos. 72 and 75078 erupt out of Keighley, 27th March 1977. Following its Bicentennial exploits of the previous year, No. 72 was still awaiting the restoration of its cab side number.

John Sagar

GREAT WESTERN RAILWAY 0-6-0 PANNIER TANKS
Nos. L89/5775 and 4612

The Great Western '57XX' pannier tanks constituted the largest class of locomotives built for service on a British railway and it is only right that these successful engines should be well represented in preservation. The Worth Valley Railway boasts two examples; No. 4612, which was purchased in 1980 from Barry scrapyard as a source of valuable spare parts, and No. 5775, restored as London Transport No. L89 in recognition of the seven years it spent in the capital after being discarded by B.R. in 1963. To date, it is the only preserved '57XX' to carry the smart London Transport maroon livery. In view of modifications carried out by L.T. this is the only authentic livery.

A redolent Great Western scene as No. 4612 stands at Tetbury with a mixed train from Kemble on 13th May 1952.

Brian Hilton

No. 5775 poses at its birthplace, Swindon, after overhaul on 28th April 1963. After thirty-four years' service on the G.W.R. and B.R. it was sold soon afterwards to London Transport. The glossy black safety valve cover seen here contrasts with the polished brass item borne by the engine in its Yorkshire exile.

Ivo Peters

A rare view of No. L89 in L.T. service passing Harrow-on-the-Hill, 14th July 1969. These pannier tanks outlived other main line steam engines in London by some three years and their nocturnal whistling and shuttling round the metropolis provoked more than one puzzled letter to **The Times.**

Keith Smith

Almost as soon as it arrived at Haworth early in 1970, No. L89 was commandeered to appear in the feature film 'The Railway Children' and painted a somewhat garish shade of brown with apocryphal Great Northern & Southern Railway lettering. No. L89 is pictured in Haworth yard minus safety valve cover.

R. Smithies

Back in lower quadrant (albeit Midland) territory, No. L89 looks very much at home as it clambers up to Damems loop, 25th August 1974.

Both: John Sagar

Spring time in the Worth Valley as No. L89 nips down from Oakworth to Damems with a Keighley train, 26th May 1975.

With its B.R. number and Merthyr shed allocation chalked on by a passing humorist, No. L89 approaches Ingrow on a sweltering 1st June 1979.

John Sagar

The cup that cheers, Keighley, 1st June 1979.

John Sagar

Appalling railway practice! No. L89 looks on resignedly as a stuntman stand-in for Bill Owen (alias 'Compo' of the BBC t.v. comedy series 'Last of the Summer Wine') dangles precariously from an overbridge near Haworth during filming, 27th June 1979. No. L89 was temporarily carrying K.W.V.R. lettering.

John Sagar

One of the most agreeable features of the Autumn Galas on the Worth Valley Railway used to be the through working of the Scottish Railway Preservation Society's rake of vintage carriages from Falkirk to Oxenhope. More stringent B.R. regulations governing the operation of privately owned vehicles now unfortunately preclude such events. Before the clamp-down, the S.R.P.S. special is shown reversing off the main line at Keighley on 6th October 1979, prior to a trip up the branch behind Nos. L89 and 5820. The B.R. track layout at Keighley was extensively remodelled in 1983.

Stuart Willetts

LONGMOOR MILITARY RAILWAY 0-6-0 SADDLE TANK No. 118 'BRUSSELS'

No. 118 **Brussels**, one of the well-known 'Austerity' 0-6-0 saddle tank locomotives, was built by Hudswell, Clarke of Leeds in 1945. Its sole owner prior to arrival at Haworth in 1971 was the War Department and it was allocated throughout its previous career to the Longmoor Military Railway, the Army's training railway in Hampshire. Initially a coal-burner, it was converted to oil firing and gained a welded steel firebox during an overhaul by the Hunslet Engine Company in the late 1950s. **Brussels** was then used to train footplate staff in the techniques of oil firing. Sad to relate, it was not an outstanding success as an oil-burner at Longmoor, probably due to lack of experience with the type of Laidlaw Drew burner fitted and inadequate draughting. This photograph depicts No. 118 at Longmoor on 16th April 1966, complete with Westinghouse air brake equipment and generator in front of the safety valve. The original name plate and crest were removed before the engine was acquired by the Worth Valley Railway, and can now be seen in the Museum of Army Transport at Beverley, Humberside. Further distinguishing features of this 'Austerity' are the unique front shunter's platforms.

Howard Malham

Another view of No. 118 at Longmoor. The cut-away saddle tank gave the engine an unfortunate lop-sided appearance, though the raised number on the buffer beam was not without appeal. Before coming north, No. 118 was initially purchased for use on the projected Longmoor tourist railway, but this scheme proved abortive. Picture taken on 30th April 1966.

Keith Smith

In dramatic style, an unnamed No. 118 gives No. 52044 a helping hand near Oxenhope, 22nd March 1975. The engine retains its original chimney and lid, but cosmetic improvements have been made to the saddle tank. During its first spell of Worth Valley running No. 118 proved to be a poor steamer. In an attempt to remedy this, an internal chimney liner was fitted.

Martin Welch

Brussels in vociferous mood between Haworth and Oxenhope, 28th December 1976. The real revolution in No. 118's level of performance came with the fitting of a Kylchap blastpipe. This necessitated the removal of the original chimney and its replacement with a stovepipe. By this date **Brussels** had also been given new nameplates.
John Sagar

A historic occasion as Nos. 118 and 5820 haul a through Ealing Broadway - Oxenhope B.R. excursion away from Keighley, 10th March 1979. The eight-coach set included two Mk. 2 vehicles, the first occasion on which such stock had traversed the branch. **Brussels** continues in fine form to the present day, its performance scaling new heights since the recent installation of an oil burner obtained from Portugal. Another fine example of Worth Valley persistence!

John Sagar

39

LANCASHIRE & YORKSHIRE RAILWAY 0-6-0 TENDER ENGINE No. 957 (B.R. No. 52044) AND 0-6-0 SADDLE TANK No. 752

These two veterans further emphasise the Worth Valley's leadership in the preservation of L. & Y.R. motive power. No. 957 is one of a 280-strong class of standard goods tender locomotives, known as 'Ironclads', constructed to the design of W. Barton Wright between 1876 and 1887. It was built by Beyer, Peacock in 1887 as one of the last batch of fifty ordered by J.A.F. Aspinall after Barton Wright's resignation. Following the introduction of his own very successful 'A' class 0-6-0 tender engines from 1889, Aspinall decided to convert most of the 'Ironclads' to saddle tanks. So successful were these conversions that, by 1900, no fewer than 230 had been modified and adopted as the standard L. & Y.R. shunting engine. No. 752 is the sole surviving example of one of these rebuilds, having started life in May 1881 in tender engine form. Nos. 957 and 752 are both extremely popular Haworth denizens, being much in demand for filming and other special events. What is more, when purchased by Tony Cox from B.R. following withdrawal in 1959, No. 957 had the distinction of being one of the very first standard gauge steam locomotives to be preserved privately in Britain. Not to be outdone, No. 752 had its moment of glory by representing the Railway at the 'Rocket 150' celebrations at Rainhill in May 1980.

The last fifty Barton Wright 0-6-0s to be built, Nos. 928-977, were unaffected by the Aspinall rebuilding and half of them survived into the B.R. era. No. 957 (alias 52044) was the last to be withdrawn, from Wakefield shed, in May 1959. The 'Ironclad' is pictured at this location on 12th April 1953, still carrying Ramsbottom safety valves. The tender emblem is of interest because, for most of its career on B.R., No. 52044 ran without such an embellishment.

R.J. Buckley

Right: Dwarfed by a much larger successor, No. 52044 lurks in the gloom of Wakefield shed in 1957. All three classes of locomotive depicted here are now, of course, represented in the Worth Valley's collection.

Tony Cox

Below: Shortly before withdrawal, No. 52044 shunts colliery sidings at Darton on the Barnsley - Crigglestone line. The Hughes pattern smokebox door was later replaced by one of the original design at the request of the engine's new owner.

Tony Cox

'Lanky' survivors near Darton in the late 1950s: No. 52044 takes refreshment from a standard L. & Y.R. water column.

Tony Cox

Masquerading as a London & North Western Railway express engine, No. 957 basks in the sunshine at Haworth in June 1969. The unsightly green livery had been applied so that the engine could star in a forthcoming Billy Wilder film, 'The Private Life of Sherlock Holmes'. Necessary mechanical work on No. 957 was carried out in collaboration with the Hunslet Engine Company.

P. Hutchinson

The following year No. 957 was painted a darker shade of green and dubbed the 'Green Dragon' to bring a touch of Victorian elegance to the feature film of E. Nesbit's 'The Railway Children'. It retained this livery for some time, as can be seen from this view of the late W. Hubert Foster performing the opening ceremony at the newly-installed Damems loop on 10th July 1971. Adjacent to the locomotive is the North Eastern Railway inspection saloon No. 1661 which itself gained fame as the 'Old Gentleman's Carriage' in the film of 'The Railway Children'.

John Sagar

Right: By 1975, No. 957 had reverted to its final plain black B.R. guise as No. 52044. It was also sufficiently healthy to be used on the Worth Valley branch on special occasions.

Martin Welch

Below: No. 52044 heads back home to Haworth after filming at Keighley on 13th March 1975. To this day I have not discovered exactly what the fireman was doing! Great events are planned for the engine's centenary in 1987, when perhaps it will be able to work passenger trains in tandem with its saddle tank sister.

John Sagar

Following the grouping, No. 752 became L.M.S. No. 11456 and, in April 1937, was sold for colliery use. It never lost its L.M.S. number, despite the application of a variegated red, green and black livery. By May 1965, however, when this picture was taken, the engine was out of use and semi-derelict at Parsonage Colliery, Leigh. It also still carried its 'L.M.S. Rebuilt Horwich 1896' plates which were stolen shortly afterwards.

Barry Hilton

No. 752 was rescued by the L. & Y.R. Saddletanks Fund in 1967. Initial restoration work was carried out at the premises of Messrs. Yates Duxbury in Bury, to which destination the saddle tank was drawn by a variety of B.R. steam engines following an itinerary which took in Kearsley, Bolton, Rochdale and Heap Bridge. With a fictitious B.R. number, Bolton shed allocation and emblem on the saddle tank, it awaits departure from Linnyshaw Moss behind '8F' 2-8-0 No. 48026 on 25th April 1968. Very early the following morning, the final leg of the journey was made behind '8F' No. 48773, now preserved on the Severn Valley Railway.

Richard S. Greenwood

Moving to Haworth in November 1971, No. 752 was first steamed the following May and, during 1972, saw limited use on works trains and brake van specials. On a dismal 3rd June 1972, No. 752 takes water at Keighley. At this time the engine carried L. & Y.R. passenger livery of black lined out in white and red. Note also the unsurfaced platform 4, the now-replaced water column and the awning still in situ on platform 3.

John Sagar

Attention is paid to No. 752's wheels at Haworth prior to its appearance in the 'Rocket 150' celebrations.

John Sagar

Above: Victorian elegance and functionalism at Bold Colliery, 26th May 1980, awaiting the Rainhill cavalcade. No. 752 now carries L. & Y.R. goods engine livery.

John Sagar

Left: Getting ready to face the public, Bold, 26th May 1980.

John Sagar

From 'Rocket 150', No. 752 ran under its own steam to Manchester Liverpool Road station for use on the internal shuttle service there during the Summer of 1980. On 13th June of that year it became the last locomotive to traverse this complex track layout at Liverpool Road. Really designed for wagon traffic, the layout was simplified immediately afterwards.

Richard S. Greenwood

No. 752 journeyed back across the Pennines in time for its one hundredth birthday party at Keighley on 18th May 1981. A 'cake', made of coal and other suitably combustible materials, was fed into the firebox before departure for Oxenhope!

John Sagar

The passing years rest lightly on No. 752 as it shunts Oakworth yard, 18th May 1981.

John Sagar

GREAT NORTHERN RAILWAY 4-4-2
No. 990
'HENRY OAKLEY'

It was a great honour when the National Railway Museum sent this famous locomotive on temporary loan to the Worth Valley Railway in 1977. No. 990, the first British Atlantic, was built at Doncaster in 1898 to the design of the great H.A. Ivatt. Withdrawn from service in 1937, this 'Klondyke' was for many years a star attraction in the old Railway Museum at York. In 1953 it emerged to double-head two special trains with 'Large Atlantic' G.N.R. No. 251 to celebrate the centenary of Doncaster Plant. No. 990 also holds the distinction of having appeared in both the 1925 and 1975 Stockton & Darlington Railway steam cavalcades. It returned to the N.R.M. at York in 1978.

As L.N.E.R. No. 3990, **Henry Oakley** leaves Kings Cross with the 13.45 Cambridge train, February 1925.

F.R. Hebron/Rail Archive Stephenson

A view of the G.N.R. Atlantics taking water at Doncaster on one of the 'Plant Centenarian' workings of September 1953. The two veterans were hustled up to no less than 80 m.p.h. near Essendine on the southbound run of 27th September.

N.R. Knight

Right: No. 990 was brought to Keighley on 20th May 1977 by No. 92220 **Evening Star.** Having deposited the Atlantic on Worth Valley territory, the '9F' duly returned to York with the Hughes 'Crab' No. 42700 which had been on loan since 1968.
Martin Welch

Below: Driver Owen of Newton Heath gets to grips with his new charge, 1st June 1977. **Henry Oakley** was very popular with Worth Valley footplate staff and it is hoped that the **Railway** has not seen the last of it!

John Sagar

Below: Raising steam at Haworth for No. 990's first day in Worth Valley revenue earning service, 1st June 1977.

John Sagar

Left: Regrettably, a high percentage of No. 990's appearances in steam on the Worth Valley were marred by torrential rain. However, conditions were much better as it arrived at Haworth with a 'down' train on 8th July 1977.

John Sagar

Below: A striking view of No. 990 running through the woods near Oxenhope in the Summer of 1977.

Robin Higgins

Like some primeval dragon emerging from its lair, No. 990 stalks Haworth yard on a Summer night in 1977.

J.R. Carter

Departure time draws near at Keighley on 10th July 1977.

John Sagar

GREAT NORTHERN RAILWAY 0-6-0 SADDLE TANK No. 1247

These robust saddle tanks were designed by H.A. Ivatt, perpetuating an earlier Stirling design. No. 1247 (B.R. No. 68846) dates from 1897 and is the last survivor of its class. For some sixty years the asthmatic bark of these engines was a common sound throughout the G.N. system as they went about their essentially workaday duties. On 20th September 1958 this engine stands at Hornsey shed, having become the first and only member of its class ever to receive the accolade of fully lined out B.R. mixed traffic livery. It was promptly exhibited in connection with the Wood Green Charter celebrations.

R.C. Riley

Purchased by Captain W.G. Smith in 1959, No. 1247 was restored at Doncaster to the full splendour of G.N.R. green livery and worked enthusiasts' specials from time to time over the ensuing years. It came to the Worth Valley in March 1965 and was put to good use on the shuttle service which the Railway occasionally ran up Haworth loop before reopening. The date is 28th May 1966.

John Sagar

Right: No. 1247 makes a splendidly nostalgic sight as it leaves Haworth with a works train on 29th May 1966. It is a pity that the locomotive did not see service on the branch after reopening.

Howard Malham

Below: Following its five-year sojourn on the Railway, No. 1247 eventually gravitated, via Tyseley, to the North York Moors Railway. Amidst the superb scenery of Newtondale it approaches Levisham with a Pickering train, 23rd April 1978. This engine is now resident at the National Railway Museum, York.

John Sagar

SWEDISH RAILWAYS 'AUSTERITY' 2-8-0 No. 1931

These locomotives were once a common sight throughout industrial Britain, no fewer than 733 of the type being employed by B.R. on heavy freight traffic. They were built from 1943 onwards under the direction of R.A. Riddles to provide a robust, cheap and simple form of motive power as part of the war effort. Although the class once seemed omnipresent, especially in the West Yorkshire area, none of the B.R. examples survived into preservation. Fortunately, a large number of these 2-8-0s had been sold abroad after the cessation of hostilities and early in 1973 No. 1931, originally sold to the Dutch Railways, was brought back to this country from Sweden, where it had been stored as part of that country's strategic reserve. Whilst in Sweden, the tender had been shortened and the engine given an all-enclosed cab for service north of the Arctic Circle. Numerous other detail modifications had also been made. Nevertheless, this 1945-built 2-8-0 gives the Worth Valley a still-recognisable example of a worthy design.

No. 1931 at Mellansjö, Sweden in September 1972. It had been in store since 1958. With its protruding headlamp, chimney, safety valves, whistle, cab roof and steps, the engine was clearly out of gauge for immediate use in Britain. Sister engine No. 1930 was stored at the same location and, although the target of a preservation bid by a group of English enthusiasts, was apparently scrapped by mistake.

Richard S. Greenwood

No. 1931 was shipped to Hull in January 1973 and is seen leaving the city, en route to Haworth.
A. McBurnie

On 24th November 1973, No. 1931 entered Worth Valley service. At that time stock for the service was still stabled at Haworth and No. 1931 gives No. 41241 a welcome shove out of the yard towards the main line. The six-coach train was being run in connection with an excursion originating from the south coast. During the preceding months, No. 1931 had received numerous modifications and the new cab roof and L.M.S. safety valves are clearly visible.

Martin Welch

Left: The 'W.D.' puts up a valiant performance with the weedkilling train at Keighley, 21st May 1974.
Martin Welch

Below: A fine portrait of No. 1931 being prepared for the day's work at Haworth shed in early April 1976.

John Fozard

Approaching Oxenhope in the torrid June of 1976, No. 1931's crew would doubtless have dispensed gladly with the enclosed cab! The second carriage in the train is the former d.m.u. buffet car which left the Railway in April 1984. No. 1931 was withdrawn for heavy repairs the following December after covering some 3,500 miles on the Worth Valley.

John Sagar

No. 1931 in close-up.

John Sagar

NORTH WESTERN GAS BOARD PECKETT 0-4-0 SADDLE TANK No. 1999

There is limited scope for the use of small industrial engines on the K.W.V.R. because of the stiff gradients and frequent heavy loadings. However, this diminutive maroon locomotive, built by Peckett of Bristol in 1941 for use at Southport Gas Works, fared as well as any before being loaned to Steamport Railway Museum at Southport in September 1974.

Left: Around 1958, No. 1999 was transferred to Darwen Gas Works and worked there until 1963. It was then stored in the open until the move to Haworth in September 1966. Despite its futuristic cab side number, the engine was evidently in a woebegone state by the end of its time at Darwen. To compound matters, a hole had been cut to release the jammed smokebox door!

Worthrail Photo Archive

58

21st April 1968 saw the Worth Valley running timetable trials. If anything, the exercise proved the unsuitability of small locomotives for regular service on the line and some six hot axle-boxes out of eight were recorded on Nos. 1999 and 2226 before Oxenhope was reached!

Ian G. Holt

Right: No. 1999 found its niche on the short-lived Summer shuttle from Haworth to Oxenhope which the Railway operated in 1970 and 1971. Here it brews up before taking its solitary coach away from Haworth, 27th August 1970.

John Sagar

Opposite page: No. 1999 is on record as having made the entire journey from Southport to Darwen under its own steam, quite a tribute to the Peckett design. It is therefore no stranger to the main line and, following mechanical work and a repaint at Haworth, its appeal to film makers also became obvious. In July 1969 it was transported to Matlock on the Midland Railway's Peak Forest main line from Ambergate Junction to Chinley, preparatory to appearing in scenes for the film of the D.H. Lawrence novel 'The Virgin and the Gypsy'. Accompanied by a Midland Railway six-wheeler and Metropolitan Railway coach, also supplied by the Worth Valley, No. 1999 is shown doing its piece for the cameras at Cromford. By all accounts it enjoyed its second brief taste of the 'big league'!

Martin Welch

I C I BARCLAY 0-4-0 SADDLE TANK
No. 2226

This sturdy blue saddle tank is a fine modern example of the work of the celebrated Scottish locomotive builders Andrew Barclay & Co. Ltd. Its whole working life, from 1946 to 1967, was spent as a shunter at I C I Huddersfield Dyestuffs Division Works. On retirement it was donated to the Society and is glimpsed at Haworth on 15th June 1968, having hauled the newly-arrived 'Crab' No. 42700 up the line from Keighley.

Howard Malham

After a boiler inspection (the engine had returned to Barclays in 1956 for a new firebox and tubes) No. 2226 was paired with No. 1999 for a round trip on the timetable trials of 21st April 1968. It steamed well and maintained a good water level, but the lack of a brick arch resulted in voluminous smoke effects. Trouble with hot bearings also indicated that it would be of limited use for service trains. Nos. 1999 and 2226 leave their mark near Mytholmes tunnel on this working.

Gavin W. Morrison

As this picture taken on 7th September 1968 testifies, the engine had been well looked after at Huddersfield. Interesting features are the open cab back and canvas sheet and the external handbrake. No. 2226 has for several years been a static exhibit in Oxenhope Museum.

Martin Welch

GREAT NORTHERN RAILWAY 'N2/2' CLASS 0-6-2 SIDE TANK No. 4744

This impressive machine was completed by the North British Locomotive Company in February 1921 to the design of H.N. Gresley. Initially numbered 1744 by the G.N.R., it was later given the numbers 4744 and 9523 by the L.N.E.R. before finishing its working life as B.R. No. 69523. The photograph shows the 'N2' in the earlier part of its L.N.E.R. career. This is the livery to which it has been restored since purchase by the Gresley Society in 1963.

Worthrail Photo Archive

Below: London and the Home Counties were the main stamping ground of the Gresley 'N2s', though they could also be seen at work in the West Riding and Scotland. Many of the class, among them No. 4744, were fitted with condensing apparatus to enable them to run through the tunnels to Moorgate. The forte of these engines was working suburban passenger and empty stock trains. No. 9523 here stands at Dunstable, where the G.N.R. line from Hatfield met the L. & N.W.R. branch from Leighton Buzzard. At the adjoining platform is Webb 0-6-2T No. 7773.

R.J. Buckley

28th May 1949 found No. 69523, in early B.R. livery, awaiting departure from Kings Cross with a Cuffley train. The 'A1' 4-6-2 had still to receive its **Pommern** nameplates.

A.C. Gilbert

Right: No. 69523 at Moorgate, 30th July 1958, about to work a train to Welwyn Garden City. Metropolitan Railway stock was still very much in evidence at that time.

R.C. Riley

Below: Botanist's paradise, preservationist's nightmare! No. 4744 in the undergrowth at Oxenhope, 31st July 1965, on arrival from Keighley with recently-delivered carriages of Metropolitan, L.N.E.R., L. & Y.R. and M.R. origins.

Howard Malham

Left: No. 4744 nears Oxenhope on 19th March 1966 with an AGM special from Haworth. The 'N2' put in only a limited mileage on the Worth Valley, being used for the last time in June 1970. During 1975 the Gresley Society took the decision to move the locomotive to the Great Central Railway at Loughborough, which was much nearer the homes of most of its members. The Gresley buffet car behind the engine is now also to be found on the G.C.R.

Robin Lush

Below: The 'N2' has established itself as a stalwart on the G.C.R. and makes a stirring sight as it pulls away from Rothley with a six-coach train on 18th April 1982.

John S. Whiteley

UNITED STATES ARMY TRANSPORTATION CORPS 'S160' CLASS 2-8-0 No. 5820

Perhaps the most enterprising scheme to rescue a steam locomotive for use on the Worth Valley was the one which brought No. 5820 all the way from Katowice in Poland to Haworth. To achieve its goal the Society had to contend not only with problems of distance. It also had to grapple with some of the more arcane workings of Polish bureaucracy. That such difficulties were overcome reflects great credit on all concerned.

John Sagar

In the period leading up to D-Day, some 800 of these American-built 2-8-0s were landed in Britain and 398 were put to work on heavy freight duties. Several actually worked through Keighley on the main line. Typical American features are the bar frames, steel firebox and extensive use of welding to reduce weight and save cost. Many 'S160s' were also delivered to other European countries and No. 5820, built by Lima, Ohio in 1945 for the U.S. Army Transportation Corps, went straight to Poland where it became No. Tr 203-474. Looking very smart after works attention, No. Tr 203-474 stands at Katowice shed in Silesia, August 1976. Before it could be used on the K.W.V.R. it was necessary to remove the out of gauge smoke deflectors and shorten the chimney. The headlamp arrangement has also been modified.

Robin Higgins

Above: Another reminder of the 'S160' at Katowice, this time taken in April 1977. In Poland the engine was painted black, with a green cab and red and white wheels and motion. Cast number plates adorned the cab and tender sides. With their self-cleaning smokeboxes, rocking grates and rocker ashpans and easy access for maintenance, the 'S160s' greatly influenced the L.M.S. designs of H.G. Ivatt and, subsequently, the B.R. standard classes.

Robin Higgins

Left: No. 5820 was hauled dead from Katowice to Szczecin and then shipped to Hull. On 7th November 1977 it was hoisted ashore using a former Hull & Barnsley Railway steam crane and a rarely-employed 100 ton capacity spreader beam.

Roger Nettleton

Above: First steamed at Haworth on 26th November 1977, the 'S160' entered revenue earning service on the Sunday of Enthusiasts' Weekend, 19th March 1978. It is pictured still in Polish-style livery heading a demonstration freight train near Oakworth.
Richard S. Greenwood

Right: The engine rapidly acquired the nickname 'Big Jim' on the Worth Valley as its haulage capacity became evident. Also on 19th March 1978, it storms away from Keighley in the company of **Fred.**
John Sagar

No. 5820 was an obvious candidate to star in the John Schlesinger-directed feature film 'Yanks', scenes for which were shot on the Railway in the Summer of 1978. In the interests of authenticity, however, it was also temporarily re-numbered 2820 to represent an 'S160' which saw service in Britain prior to D-Day. Filming necessitated the turning of locomotives on the triangle at Shipley and No. 5820 was given special permission to work over B.R. for this purpose. Bowling along at 40 m.p.h., it plunges into Bingley tunnel on 21st June 1978. By this time the engine had been painted grey with white lettering.

John Sagar

Below: Nos. 5820 and 118 depart from Oxenhope with the return special to Ealing Broadway, 10th March 1979.

John Sagar

In characteristic fashion, No. 5820 hurries up the valley between Haworth and Oxenhope on 4th April 1981.

John Sagar

Below: Feeding time for 'Big Jim'.　John Sagar

Injector and pipework detail on No. 5820.　John Sagar

LONDON MIDLAND & SCOTTISH RAILWAY CLASS '8F' 2-8-0 No. 8431

The first of Stanier's 2-8-0 heavy freight locomotives for the L.M.S. appeared in 1935 and by 1939 the class was 126 strong. During World War Two there was a pressing need for heavy freight power to keep traffic moving throughout Britain and in foreign fields. This Stanier design was adopted by the War Department as a standard and by 1946 the class was 852 strong. Under the auspices of the Ministry of Supply, production of the '8Fs' spread from the L.M.S. workshops to Swindon on the G.W.R., Doncaster and Darlington on the L.N.E.R. and Ashford, Brighton and Eastleigh on the S.R. Private firms such as Beyer, Peacock, North British and Vulcan Foundry added their weight to the building programme. A few members of the class remain at work in Turkey to this day and several others were lost at sea during the war.

The Worth Valley's '8F', No. 8431, was built at Swindon in 1944 and turned out in L.M.S. livery. It was allocated to Gloucester on the G.W.R. until 1947 and then transferred to the L.M.S. depot at Royston in Yorkshire. On 19th September 1948 it was on shed at Toton. The numbers are high up on the cab sides, above the power classification and level with the tender lettering.

H.C. Casserley

In 1955 No. 48431, as it had become, returned to B.R. Western Region, where it was to remain for the rest of its working life. Initially shedded at Bristol, it later moved to London Old Oak Common. On Sunday 11th September 1960 the '8F' wheels a heavy 'up' coal train through Oxford.

M. Mensing

... study of the immaculate No. 48431 at Old Oak Common, 24th September 1961. Adjacent to it is 'Hall' 4-6-0 No. ...984 **Albrighton Hall**.

R.J. Blenkinsop

...o. 48431 ended its days in B.R. service at Bath Green Park shed, probably working trains over the Somerset and ...orset route. Here it simmers outside the shed on 12th February 1964.

Ivo Peters

Following withdrawal in 1964, No. 48431 was despatched to Barry scrapyard in South Wales. Purchased in March 1971 as a long-term restoration project, it did at least come complete with coupling and connecting rods. These are seen being lowered to ground level at Haworth on 29th May 1972, shortly after the engine's arrival.

John Sagar

Such was the dedication of the team working on it that the '8F' was steamed by 1st January 1975 and placed in service the following December. Restoration was to L.M.S. plain black, but with the cab side numbers in the lower position. In June 1978 it even ventured down the Aire valley to turn on the Shipley triangle in conjunction with the filming of 'Yanks'. On the 21st of that month it negotiates Shipley Bradford Junction, heading back to Keighley.

John Sagar

No. 8431 takes a lightweight freight train up to Oxenhope, 31st March 1979.

John Sagar

Above: Wintry prospect at Oxenhope, 20th December 1981. Only one Stanier '8F' was fitted with steam heat on B.R., but the Worth Valley soon put the equipment on for winter working.

Richard S. Greenwood

Right: Getting ready for the road, Haworth, 16th July 1983.
John Sagar

Below: A majestic No. 8431 draws into Oxenhope with an early afternoon train from Keighley, 1st August 1983. The modified arrangement of the vacuum ejector at the front of the boiler is a mid-1950s B.R. Western Region feature. As a result, No. 8431's livery is not strictly correct at present.
John Sagar

BRITISH RAILWAYS 'WEST COUNTRY' CLASS 4-6-2 No. 34092 'CITY OF WELLS'

This three cylinder 'air smoothed' Bulleid Pacific is a major attraction on the Worth Valley Railway and a fitting tribute to its creator, probably the most forward-looking steam locomotive designer Britain has ever seen. Built at Brighton in 1949, No. 34092 spent most of its B.R. career hauling prestigious trains between London Victoria and the Kent coast. After covering 502,864 miles, **City of Wells** was withdrawn from service at Salisbury in November 1964 and sent to moulder in the locomotive graveyard at Barry. It was purchased by three Worth Valley members in 1971 and, after a nine-year restoration programme, **City of Wells** made its triumphant return to active service in March 1980, confounding the cynics who had confidently predicted that it would never succeed in pulling more than its own tender up the steep branch! Delight was unconfined when, some twenty months later, further work enabled it to join the elite group of steam locomotives permitted to haul passenger trains over B.R. Since then it has pleased thousands far and wide and is a magnificent standard-bearer for the Railway.

Left: The Bulleid look comes to Keighley, 1st April 1980.
John Sagar

Below: An early picture of No. 34092, less than a month old, approaching Shorncliffe with a boat train in September 1949. The locomotive carries short **Wells** nameplates, but these are covered over awaiting the formal naming ceremony which took place at Wells, Somerset on 25th November 1949. The name was expanded to **City of Wells** the following March. No. 34092 was equipped from new with a 5,500 gallon capacity tender and also boasted round hinged covers to the sand filler chutes.
Rev. A.C. Cawston: D.T. Cobbe collection

Twenty-eight years separate these views of **City of Wells** under repair at Bricklayers Arms Works on 2nd April 1955 and Haworth on 27th August 1983. Keeping express steam locomotives in the prime of condition is a never-ending task.

Brian Morrison and John Sagar

From 1949 to 1961, No. 34092 was allocated to Stewarts Lane depot at Battersea where it was one of the 'top link' engines. It found frequent employment on the renowned 'Golden Arrow' Pullman train, as well as on special workings conveying visiting Heads of State to and from the capital. On 27th April 1956 it hurries through the pouring rain at Streatham carrying Russian leaders Khrushchev and Bulganin to Portsmouth on the first leg of their return journey to Moscow. The train was routed via Herne Hill and Dorking before heading down the mid-Sussex line to the coast and then west to Portsmouth.

Stanley Creer

City of Wells was selected for another important duty on 16th July 1956 when it ferried King Feisal of Iraq from Dover to Victoria at the start of his state visit. The train is seen at speed near West enhanger. Note the superb appearance of the loco- motive, with burnished buffers, coupling, frame ends and tyres – even on the tender!

Peter J. Bawcut

No. 34092 in classic setting, taking water at Stewarts Lane shed on 25th May 1958. It is still paired with its original tender, though the sandbox filler doors have been modified and the fairing in front of the cylinders has gone. There is also more visible conduit to the lower front electric lights than on the engine as running at present. **R.C. Riley**

No. 34092 stayed at Stewarts Lane until the elimination of steam from the London-Ashford-Dover main line in the late Spring of 1961. In the twilight of its days on the South Eastern Division of the Southern Region, it runs along Folkestone Warren, in the shadow of the chalk cliffs, with a special Pullman train from Victoria to Dover Marine. Date of the picture is 15th April 1961, and the **overhead** warning flashes seem most inappropriate! **D.T. Cobbe**

'West Country' Pacific in decline. Relegated to freight work and with badly leaking cylinder drain taps, **City of Wells** passes an eastbound 'S15' 4-6-0 No. 30831 near Templecombe on 4th November 1961, shortly after its transfer to Salisbury depot. The battery box for No. 34092's a.w.s. gear is prominent above the buffer beam. Although it was the penultimate unmodified Bulleid Pacific to receive a general overhaul at Eastleigh Works, in November 1962, its days at Salisbury were numbered.

Tony Richardson

An unkempt **City of Wells** chatters away from Wilton in August 1963 with a westbound express. During its final visit to Eastleigh the engine received a number of detail changes. The early outside big end fastening was replaced by the four-stud version, the single piece crosshead and piston rod was changed to the later coned, jointed assembly on the two outside cylinders, and the conduit to the front electric lights was re-routed. It also lost its large tender to a modified Pacific and was given the 4,500 gallon tender from No. 34051 **Winston Churchill**. From No. 34071 onwards the Bulleid light Pacifics were built with 9′ wide cabs and tenders as opposed to the 8′6″ of the earlier engines; hence the discrepancy between engine and tender evident in this and later views.

Tony Richardson

Right: The long, slow process of restoration under way at Haworth in the Summer of 1974. Note how the casing is carried on ribs of channel section attached to brackets off the main frames.

John Sagar

Left: Injector detail on No. 34092 during restoration.　　　John Sagar

Below: In best Southern fashion, No. 34092 briefly ran unnamed before the official renaming ceremony performed by the Mayor of Wells on 1st April 1980. On 23rd March that year it pilots No. 43924 away from Keighley.

John Sagar

As in its Stewarts Lane days, **City of Wells** continues to be rostered for special duties. 21st April 1982 saw it taking part in a publicity event organized in conjunction with the Eurovision Song Contest held in Harrogate. Behind the engine are two latter-day Pullmans from the National Railway Museum.

John Sagar

Right: After mechanical and boiler attention at Steamtown, Carnforth in 1980-81, No. 34092 was given two opportunities to prove itself on the main line. The second of these was scheduled for 12th December 1981, a day of almost unprecedented cold with over twenty degrees Celsius of frost being recorded at several places in England. At midnight on 11th December 1981, **City of Wells** shivers at Carnforth with braziers attempting to prevent pipework from freezing: a hand-held exposure using car headlights for illumination and a block of ice as a tripod!

John Sagar

Below: The engine gave a splendid account of itself on this northern 'Golden Arrow' of 12th December 1981 and was awarded its main line ticket. Unfortunately, the weather conditions prevented the train from going beyond Skipton and the return to Carnforth had to be made tender-first. **City of Wells** provides a breathtaking spectacle as it approaches Clapham.

Dr. L.A. Nixon

The harsh realities of steam preservation.

John Sagar

To date, No. 34092 has worked main line specials to and from such diverse places as Carlisle, Scarborough and Maryport. Probably its most thrilling run so far was on the 'Cumbrian Coast Express' of 28th July 1982, when some twenty minutes of a late departure were made up between Sellafield and Carnforth. Sound effects were tremendous throughout, as was the coal consumption! No. 34092 races along the single-line section from Whitehaven.

Dr. W.A. Sharman

A shot which captures the very essence of the Settle and Carlisle. With electric lights glowing, **City of Wells** leaves Garsdale in a heavy squall on the north-bound 'Cumbrian Mountain Pullman' of 13th November 1982.

D.J. Fowler

Right: Steam interloper at Scarborough, 26th July 1983. Ten years ago who would ever have thought such a scene possible? The headboard, in a style introduced by B.R. Southern Region from 1953, was specially commissioned by No. 34092's owners.

John Sagar

Below: Another famous train whose name is perpetuated by **City of Wells** is the 'Night Ferry'. Late on 10th December 1983, after working a special down from Carlisle, No. 34092 awaits departure from Keighley with a pseudo-'Night Ferry' composed of former B.R. Mk.1 sleeping cars. The sleepers were destined for volunteer accommodation at Haworth and the headboard had been loaned by the N.R.M., York.

John Sagar

BRITISH RAILWAYS CLASS '2MT' 2-6-2 SIDE TANK No. 41241

H.G. Ivatt's highly successful '2MT' 2-6-2 tank locomotives were first introduced on the L.M.S. in 1946 to replace obsolete motive power on secondary duties. In No. 41241 the K.W.V.R. possesses the ideal modern branch line passenger engine. Motor-fitted examples of the class worked push-and-pull trains over the line for several years up to June 1960. No. 41241 was built after nationalisation, emerging from Crewe Works in 1949. Its early years were spent working over the Somerset and Dorset line. On 21st June 1952 No. 41241 and Ivatt '4MT' No. 43039 await departure from Bath Green Park station with the 10.00 for Bristol. No. 41241 retained this livery of lined black with small early B.R. emblem until withdrawal. The Somerset and Dorset was closed in 1966 and Bath Green Park station is now a Sainsbury's supermarket.

Ivo Peters

No. 41241 subsequently moved to Wellington shed in Shropshire and featured regularly on passenger trains over the line to Crewe. It is shown standing at Crewe in the early 1960s with an early afternoon Wellington branch local.

Martin Welch

Another glimpse of No. 41241 on the Crewe-Wellington line, this time in G.W.R. territory at Market Drayton.

R.J. Buckley

A presentable No. 41241 stands under the wires at Crewe.

N.R. Knight

No. 41241's last port of call in B.R. service was Skipton shed, from where it was purchased by the late Ronald Ainsworth and W. Hubert Foster early in 1967. It ran the short distance from Skipton to Haworth under its own steam on 18th March 1967. Shortly before leaving Skipton it was shunted onto the turntable by B.R. 'Britannia' Pacific No. 70027, formerly named **Rising Star**. On the death of Ronald Ainsworth, and largely through the generosity of Hubert Foster, ownership of No. 41241 passed to the Society.

the late W. Hubert Foster

Above: Professional attention was paid to
No. 41241's paintwork at Haworth and it
soon emerged resplendent in maroon,
lined out in black and yellow, with K.W.V.R
and the Society crest on the tank sides. In
this form it made an imposing sight as it
double-headed the reopening special on
29th June 1968 with No. 72.

Howard Malham

Left: Construction work on the new
Damems loop proceeds apace in early
Spring 1971 as No. 41241 picks its way past
with an Oxenhope train. The stock is an
unusual mixture of L.N.E.R., L.M.S. and
Metropolitan Railway vehicles.

Martin Welch

No. 41241 was invited to participate in the Shildon cavalcade of 31st August 1975 and made the journey over B.R. under its own power. Earlier that month it eases past Shipley Bingley Junction with the Railway's Southern brake, L.N.E.R. metal-bodied van No. E70442E and an L.M.S. 'B T K' (now on the Strathspey Railway) in tow.

John S. Whiteley

No. 41241 on the internal shuttle service at Shildon, 28th August 1975, giving rear-end assistance to 'Modified Hall' 4-6-0 No. 6960 **Raveningham Hall.**

Gavin W. Morrison

Left: A steady hand at Oxenhope, March 1980, during the engine's reversion to B.R. black livery.

John Sagar

Below: The immaculate No. 41241 stands at Haworth on 16th March 1980. Where Ivatt tanks are concerned many people clearly feel that black is best!

John Sagar

On 26th September 1982, No. 41241 left the Railway for firebox attention at the Resco workshops at Erith, Kent. Before its return north, and following test runs, it put in two days' work on the Kent & East Sussex Railway. On New Year's Day 1983 it performed shunting duties between Tenterden and Hexden Bridge. The next day it powered three passenger trains from Tenterden Town to Wittersham Road. On 2nd January 1983 the 'Ivatt' climbs Tenterden bank with the 'Wealden Pullman'. Banking assistance is provided by Manning, Wardle 0-6-0ST No. 14 **Charwelton**.

Brian Stephenson

No. 41241 nears Tenterden with the last train of the day on 2nd January 1983. A week later it was back home.

Brian Stephenson

MIDLAND RAILWAY CLASS '1F' 0-6-0 SIDE TANK No. 41708

This venerable Johnson-designed tank engine, built at Derby as long ago as 1880, was retained as a works shunter at Staveley Ironworks until the mid-1960s and only condemned at the end of 1966. No. 41708 and its colleagues (comprising other '1F' tanks, M.R. 'OF' 0-4-0 tanks and L.M.S./B.R. 'OF' 0-4-0 saddle tanks) attracted many photographers to Staveley. These two views of the 'half cab' taking water and shunting on 9th May 1964 show why.

Howard Malham

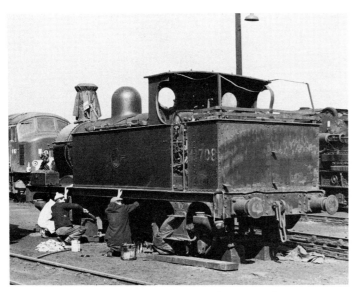

Purchased from B.R. by the Midland '1F' Fund, No. 41708 had a momentous journey from Canklow shed to Keighley. It ran four hot axle-boxes en route and was briefly laid up at Leeds Holbeck depot, where the wheels were removed and the engine placed on wooden blocks. The '1F' receives attention from Worth Valley members during its sojourn in Leeds, Spring 1967.

Howard Malham

Reaching the Railway on 15th June 1967, the 'half cab' promised to bring a welcome Midland flavour to a Midland branch. Engines of this class were once a common sight in the Worth Valley. However, it soon became clear that No. 41708 was in very run-down condition and steamings were few and far between. Here the '1F' simmers in Haworth yard, September 1970, looking very smart as L.M.S. No. 1708.

John Sagar

On 18th April 1971, No. 1708 made three round trips over the branch as pilot to No. 41241. This was the only occasion it appeared on Worth Valley service trains and this photograph, taken from the signal gantry at Oakworth, is of considerable rarity value. No. 1708 was moved away by its trustees in December 1974 and can now be found at the Midland Railway Centre, Butterley.

John S. Whiteley

LONDON MIDLAND & SCOTTISH RAILWAY CLASS '5MT' 2-6-0s Nos. 42700 and 42765

George Hughes, first Chief Mechanical Engineer of the L.M.S., drew up his design for a new 2-6-0 mixed traffic locomotive shortly before his retirement in 1925. His successor, Sir Henry Fowler, saw the concept through to completion and the class eventually totalled 245 engines. With their massive-looking cylinders set high up and at a rakish angle to clear Midland Division platforms, they had a distinctive, slightly ungainly appearance and were commonly known as 'Crabs'. The class was active almost to the end of B.R. steam. Since then two of them have, at various times, graced the Worth Valley.

The pioneer 'Crab' No. 13000 in works grey at Horwich in 1926. The engine was taken to Derby for application of the 'Derby red' top coat. No. 13000 later became L.M.S. No. 2700 and B.R. No. 42700. The tender, which was kept until withdrawal, is unique for a 'Crab' in that it has no coal space doors.

B.R., L.M.R.

The 'Crabs' were extremely successful locomotives and equally at home on passenger and freight work. No. 42700 was a familiar sight in the North West for many years and was allocated to Bury shed at the time this picture was taken. On 1st June 1963 it heads a Todmorden-Southport excursion between Rochdale and Castleton.

Barry Hilton

Sprinting down the West Coast main line at Fowler Lane, south of Farington Junction, on the evening of 1st July 1964, No. 42700 returns a special from Blackpool to Rochdale.

W.H. Ashcroft

On withdrawal from B.R. service in March 1966, No. 42700 was retained for eventual display as part of the national collection and stored in the disused engine shed at Hellifield. Pending some decision as to its long-term future, it was sent to the Worth Valley on temporary loan, reaching Keighley on 11th June 1968. No. 42700 was found to be in reasonable condition and entered passenger service on 20th October 1968. Creative use of flare adds to this picture of the 'Crab' on a filming assignment for Granada t.v. at Keighley late on 20th November 1968.

Robin Lush

Above: Attempts were made to tidy up the engine's dowdy paintwork at Haworth. Restoration to L.M.S. plain black livery was almost complete by 14th December 1968 when No. 2700 hauled a five-coach 'Santa Special' up the line. Considerable difficulty was experienced with greasy rails, as illustrated by the hand-sanding in progress between Ingrow and Damems!

Martin Welch

Left: This fine engine left Haworth for the N.R.M., York in May 1977. For some time prior it had been a static exhibit in Oxenhope Museum, where B.R. mixed traffic livery was applied. The N.R.M., however, favoured a return to L.M.S. lined black. No. 2700 stands by the turntable in the locomotive hall at York, May 1979.

John Sagar

The loss of No. 42700 was compensated for by the arrival of No. 42765 at Ingrow in April 1978. This engine was built at Crewe in 1927 as L.M.S. No. 13065 and, after a brief spell working from Leicester shed, spent a considerable period at Manchester Belle Vue. In June 1928 it takes a Belle Vue – Fleetwood special over Salwick troughs. No. 13065 carried crimson lake livery until 1931.

Frank Dean

No. 2765 came to grief just outside West Hampstead station on 23rd February 1937 whilst heading an overnight express freight from Manchester to London. A crane from Kentish Town, drawn by '4F' No. 4243, swings into action to clear the debris. Although No. 2765, which was travelling at speed, tore up the track for some distance, it embedded itself in the earth and remained upright. Fortunately there were no casualties.

BBC Hulton Picture Library

A highly evocative picture of Midland '4F' No. 43835 (with 'L M S' still visible on its tender) and No. 42765 (in early British Railways livery) as they pass through Woodville, near Ashby-de-la-Zouch, on 25th June 1949. The train is the 10.25 Blackpool-Desford.

Real Photographs

Later in its life No. 42765 was a Fleetwood engine. 13th May 1964 saw it pausing at the south end of Preston station with an 'up' fish train from its home town. Engine now fitted with a.w.s. gear.

Frank Dean

One of the last 'Crabs' to remain in service, No. 42765 worked out its final days on B.R. from Birkenhead depot. On 1st August 1964 it makes a lively departure from Crewe with a 'down' express for the Chester line.
Real Photographs

Withdrawal from service came in December 1966 and No. 42765 was sent to Barry scrapyard. Rescued by Andy Wilson, it stands at Ingrow on 8th April 1978, the grim weather almost presaging the difficulties awaiting the restoration team. Since then, good progress has been made towards returning the Worth Valley's second 'Crab' to steam. The intention is that one day it should join **City of Wells** as a main line runner.

Howard Malham

MIDLAND RAILWAY CLASS '4F' 0-6-0 No. 43924

A special place is reserved for No. 43924 in locomotive history because it was the first engine to be exhumed from Barry scrapyard and returned to steam. That milestone was passed in 1970 and since then the '4F' has been a great asset to the Worth Valley Railway.

Fowler's '4F' freight locomotives were first introduced on the Midland in 1911 and 197 had been built by the time of the grouping in 1923, five of them for the Somerset & Dorset Joint Railway. The L.M.S. constructed a further 575. This shed scene is thought to have been taken at Kentish Town about 1922. Note the distinctive Midland tender complete with coal rails. The engine still has tail rods on the pistons, with covers projecting through the front buffer beam. Other interesting details are the tall chimney and dome and Ramsbottom safety valves.

H.C. Casserley collection

Built at Derby in 1920 and withdrawn as B.R. No. 43924 in 1965, the '4F' spent its final years of service in the Gloucester area. This memory of No. 43924 at Gloucester shed on 27th September 1953 provides much to please locomotive historians. The engine is now paired with a higher-sided tender and sports patches on the buffer beam where the tail rods used to be. A lower 'standard' chimney has been fitted, but the tall dome survives. Ramsbottom safety valves have given way to the Ross Pop variety and there is a spiked finial on the whistle.

Brian Hilton

No. 43924 negotiates Over junction with a Yate-Gloucester ballast train, 1st August 1958.

Michael Jackson

Proof that the humble No. 43924 did occasionally graduate to passenger work is given by this view of it at Tewkesbury on 30th July 1960 with a train from Ashchurch to Upton-on-Severn.

Rae Montgomery

The '4F' approaching Gloucester in the early 1960s. By then it had acquired a shorter dome, new buffer beam without patches and final B.R. emblem.

B.G. Staddon

First restored as L.M.S. No. 3924, the former Barry engine makes one of its first runs under its own steam at Haworth, 4th October 1970.

Martin Welch

Right: Dominated by the landscape, No. 3924 curves away from Damems loop, 25th August 1974.

John Sagar

Left: In September 1971, No. 3924 was briefly disguised as '4F' No. 43967 to appear in a proposed film paying tribute to Driver John Axon, G.C., killed in the Chapel-en-le-Frith accident of 9th February 1957. The Severn Valley's '8F' 2-8-0 No. 8233 was renumbered 48188 for the same film.

Robin Higgin

Above: 1976 saw the appearance of the '4F' in early B.R. livery, which it retained until Summer 1983. The Worth Valley scored a 'first' in applying this livery to a preserved steam engine. No. 43924 turns back the clock at Keighley, 4th April 1976.

John Sagar

Right: The '4Fs' were hardly renowned for speed and a small dog takes No. 43924 on for pace as it jogs through Oakworth with a 'down' goods, 18th March 1978.

John Sagar

Above: Raindrops keep falling on my head .. : No. 43924's canvas sheet is indispensable in the unpredictable Yorkshire climate. Worth Valley super power near Haworth, 1st April 1979.

John Sagar

Opposite page: In Summer 1983 the engine's tender tank became life-expired and it was loaned the coal rail tender from No. 42765. At the same time, it was given overhead warning flashes and a yellow stripe as applied by B.R. in the mid-1960s to steam locomotives not permitted to run under the electric wires south of Crewe. This was another Worth Valley 'first' in preservation. No. 43924 strides confidently away from Keighley, 22nd October 1983.

John Sagar

Boiler washout for No. 43924.   **John Sagar**

LONDON MIDLAND & SCOTTISH RAILWAY CLASS '5MT' 4-6-0s Nos. 45025 and 45212

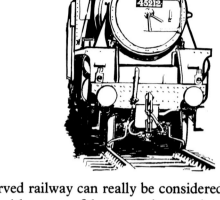

No. 45025 at Copy Pit, between Burnley and Todmorden, in the mid-1960s. This engine was purchased on withdrawal from B.R. service by the late Mr. W.E.C. Watkinson. It was then loaned to the Society for a period to ascertain its mechanical condition. Built by Vulcan Foundry for the L.M.S. in 1934, No. 45025 still carried an original domeless boiler at withdrawal.　**C. Mills**

No preserved railway can really be considered complete without one of these great locomotives on its books. The 'Black Fives' were probably the most successful steam engines ever to run in Britain. They went almost everywhere and could do anything from branch freight to express passenger work. By 1951 no fewer than 842 of them had been built.

The final celebrated duty of the 'Black Fives' was the unofficially-named 'Belfast Boat Express' from Manchester to Heysham and return. No. 45025 was a regular on this working and was in charge on 5th May 1968, the last day of steam operation. Here it stands at Bolton Trinity Street on 18th April 1968 with the 20.55 Manchester-Heysham.

A.C. Gilbert

No. 45025 was put to work as soon as it arrived on the Worth Valley in the Summer of 1969. It was still in B.R. livery, but with painted smokebox number. On 17th July 1969 it leaves Keighley, unusually working out of platform 3 because of relaying work on platform 4 road. The gutted Keighley West box has since been demolished.

Howard Malham

Below: This Stanier 'Black Five' was meticulously repainted as L.M.S. No. 5025 in 1970, the job even including white tyres for official photographs! On 12th September that year the Mayor of Keighley and members of the Council visited the Railway and the special train was headed by No. 5025, seen here at Mytholmes.

John Sagar

No. 5025 left Haworth for its new home on the Strathspey Railway in Scotland in December 1974. Occasionally it emerges to work B.R. steam specials in the Highlands, where these locomotives once reigned supreme. It is depicted making a vigorous departure from Perth with a special to Aviemore, 6th July 1981.

John S. Whiteley

Like No. 45025, the Railway's own 'Black Five' No. 45212 survived to the very end of steam on B.R., being withdrawn from Lostock Hall shed in August 1968. For much of its life it was a Fleetwood engine and was based there when photographed on excursion duty at Bridlington, 12th July 1959. No. 45212 carried a boiler with separate dome and top feed at this time.

106

N. Skinner

Above: A scene which brings back many happy memories: No. 45212 rests outside the typical L. & Y.R. straight shed at Lower Darwen in the early 1960s. By then a domeless boiler had been fitted.
Worthrail Photo Archive

Right: No. 45212 enters the now closed and demolished station at Garstang and Catterall with a Manchester-Barrow stopping train, 20th July 1963.
Ian G. Holt

The 'Black Five' parked at Carlisle Kingmoor on 10th September 1966 following a mishap. Its cab remains slightly askew to this day. Note the boiler with separate dome and top feed and the vertical strips near the front of the tender. These served to secure canvas sheeting during snowplough duty.

A.C. Gilbert

Restored to health, No. 45212 takes an I C I soda ash train through Lancaster on 17th June 1967. The smokebox lamp bracket has been lowered and the bottom middle bracket placed off-centre for added safety in overhead electrified territory.

A.C. Gilbert

On the last day of steam in ordinary B.R. service, No. 45212 awaits departure from Preston at 20.48 on 3rd August 1968 with the Blackpool portion of the 17.05 from Euston. This was the penultimate steam-hauled passenger service train on B.R. The last was the 21.25 Preston-Liverpool Exchange, headed by No. 45318.

Robin Lush

Right: It fell to No. 45212 to perform what was positively the last steam passenger duty in ordinary B.R. service. On the morning of 4th August 1968 it shunted sleeping cars from Euston into the bay at Preston and then supplied steam heat.

Keith Smith

Below: Early days for this 'Black Five' on the K.W.V.R. at Oxenhope, Easter 1969. The livery is dingy B.R. black enlivened by an L.M.S.-style smokebox number plate.

Martin Welch

Left: By the Spring of 1970, No. 45212 had been repainted in B.R. lined black with the Worth Valley crest on the tender. It also carried an early B.R./L.M.R.-style smokebox number plate and is pictured at the new Damems loop on 10th July 1971.

John Sagar

Below: Oiling round on No. 45212.

Robin Higgins

No. 45212 heads out of a storm at Oakworth in October 1975.

John Sagar

The locomotive as finally running on the Worth Valley, with early B.R. 'ferret and dartboard' tender emblem and lamp brackets unchanged from B.R. days. No. 45212 leaves Haworth on 7th June 1977. It was withdrawn from service soon afterwards pending extensive and costly repairs.

John Sagar

LONDON MIDLAND & SCOTTISH RAILWAY 'ROYAL SCOT' CLASS 4-6-0 No. 46115 'SCOTS GUARDSMAN'

As rebuilt by Sir William Stanier, these 4-6-0s were widely acknowledged as the finest express passenger 4-6-0s in the country. They were the mainstay of express services over L.M.S. lines before and after nationalisation. By 1st June 1963, however, No. 46115 **Scots Guardsman** had been relegated to lesser duties, as shown by this picture of it at Castleton with a Manchester Exchange-Bridlington special. First two coaches in the train are a Stanier articulated twin.

Barry Hilton

This engine was built for the L.M.S. in 1927 by the North British Locomotive Company. It was rebuilt in 1947, at which time it became the first rebuilt 'Scot' to acquire smoke deflectors. On 10th August 1964 No. 46115 arrives at Carlisle Citadel with the 07.00 from Glasgow.

John S. Whiteley

On 13th February 1965 Hellifield witnesses the passage of **Scots Guardsman** with a 'Scot Commemorative' rail tour. Unfortunately, strong winds prevented the hoped-for fast ascent to Blea Moor. No. 46115 was the last member of the class to be condemned, in December 1965, and was bought for preservation by the late Mr. R.A. Bill. After a period in store at Carlisle Kingmoor, it journeyed south to Keighley on 11th August 1966. Note the yellow stripe on the cab.

Howard Malham

No. 46115 was never steamed at Haworth, its sheer size meaning that it was placed well down in the list of restoration priorities. Moreover, its axle-loading would have precluded any regular use. It nevertheless proved a very popular exhibit.

the late Eric Treacy

May 1969 saw the transfer of No. 46115 to the Dinting Railway Centre and its repainting in the 1946 L.M.S. express livery of black with maroon and straw lining. In the Autumn of 1978 **Scots Guardsman** made an all too brief return to the main line, hauling two specials between Guide Bridge and York. Stricter B.R. boiler regulations prevented further trips. The beautifully restored three cylinder 4-6-0 stands at Chinley on 14th October.

Richard Stevens

No. 6115 speeds through the Autumn mist at Hathersage, 11th November 1978.

John Sagar

LONDON MIDLAND & SCOTTISH RAILWAY CLASS '3F' 0-6-0 SIDE TANK No. 47279

422 of these standard L.M.S. shunting locomotives, commonly known as 'Jinties', were constructed between 1924 and 1930. The Worth Valley's example emerged from Vulcan Foundry, Newton-le-Willows, in 1924. Initially numbered L.M.S. No. 7119, it later became their No. 7279 and finally B.R. No. 47279. Many 'Jinties' lived to a ripe age, turning their hand to occasional passenger and freight work as well as shunting. Given their derivation from the earlier Midland '1F' and '3F' tank engine designs, it is particularly appropriate that one of these durable locomotives should be resident at Haworth.

No. 47279 stands at Bedford shed in March 1961. The locomotive had a Fowler 'Jinty' boiler at this time. It is thought that this must have been exchanged for its present Johnson boiler during 1961-62.

R.E. Burdon

No. 47279 was stationed for many years at Bedford and Wellingborough depots, moving later to Workington and retiring from Sutton Oak, St. Helens. On 18th September 1961 it could be found simmering in the yard alongside Mitchells and Butlers Brewery, Bedford.

M. Mensing

By the time this picture was taken at Wellingborough shed in 1963, No. 47279 had acquired the later B.R. emblem. It is also interesting to note that its boiler belonged originally to an M.R. Johnson-type 'Jinty' since it still bears the original water feed clack-box inlets just in front of the water tanks. To conform with other L.M.S. '3F' tank locomotives the water delivery inlet was eventually transferred to the firebox back-plate.

Sharpe Photographic

A forlorn No. 47279 stands at Ingrow after extraction from Barry scrapyard, 16th August 1979. Since then excellent progress has been made with its restoration.

John Sagar

'AUSTERITY' 0-6-0 SADDLE TANKS
No. 68077 and 'FRED'

These two locomotives are coal-burning versions of No. 118 **Brussels**, but there are certain important differences between No. 68077 and **Fred.** The former is still virtually in its original condition. It was built by Andrew Barclay in 1947 and bought almost immediately by the L.N.E.R., becoming their No. 8077. Along with 74 other engines of this type it formed B.R. class 'J94' and is known to have worked at Hornsey, Boston and Colwick. In late 1962 it was purchased from B.R. service by the N.C.B. (South Yorkshire Area) and renumbered No. 14. In need of heavy repairs, it has not so far worked on the Worth Valley. **Fred,** on the other hand, spent nearly all its working life at collieries in the Wigan, Leigh and Walkden areas of Lancashire. Built by Robert Stephenson and Hawthorn in 1945, it was rebuilt in 1964 with an underfeed stoker and patent producer gas system as well as a multiple-nozzle blastpipe and new chimney. The underfeed stoker has been removed since **Fred** came to Haworth, but otherwise the engine remains largely as rebuilt. It has acquitted itself well in passenger service. **Fred** was hauled 'dead' to Keighley in freight trains over Christmas 1968.

When delivered to the Railway in 1971, No. 68077 still carried its
B.R. smokebox number plate.

Martin Welch

117

Above: No. 68077 as repainted black for static display at Oxenhope.
John Sagar

Left: Fred poses outside Bickershaw colliery engine shed following overhaul at Walkden in early 1951.
Worthrail Photo Archive

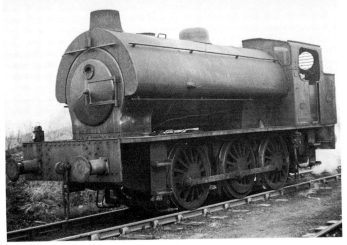

A grubby **Fred** in rebuilt condition at Walkden in January 1968. It is named after the late Mr. Fred Hilton, erstwhile locomotive superintendent of the Manchester Collieries railway system.

Ian G. Holt

Centre: Fred and No. L89 run round their train at Keighley, 19th July 1970. The pannier tank is in 'Railway Children' brown, but with 'Worth Valley' on the tanks.

Martin Welch

Left: Fred beats out a staccato rhythm near Haworth, 2nd January 1977. The shutter on the smokebox door is used to vary the vacuum produced and so reduce the draught on the fire.

John Sagar

BRITISH RAILWAYS CLASS 'J72' 0-6-0 SIDE TANK No. 69023 'JOEM'

This North Eastern Railway design dates from 1898, but the last 28 members of the 'J72' class, Nos. 69001-69028, were not constructed until 1950-51. Essentially shunting engines, they also performed station pilot duties at such places as York and Newcastle, where selected examples were painted green. No. 69023 rests in Gateshead roundhouse, 30th May 1964.

Maurice S. Burns

Below: Along with No. 69005, this engine was transferred to B.R. departmental stock for a time and renumbered No. 59. In 1966 it was bought by Ronald Ainsworth, who named it **Joem** in memory of his parents Joseph and Emmeline. On 16th October that year the 'J72' passes Thwaites Junction on the last leg of its trip from Heaton to Keighley. Pullman car No. 84 had been collected at York.

Howard Malham

Above: The Railway obtained special dispensation to run a Worth Valley 'Centenary Special' on 13th April 1967, but it was not possible to carry passengers. No. 69023, in freshly applied pseudo-N.E.R. colours, headed the four coach train and No. 41241 provided assistance from the rear.

Robin Lush

Right: This picture, taken from the footbridge at Haworth in the Summer of 1969, shows the obtrusive 'Class J72' which **Joem** wore on its buffer beam whilst on the Worth Valley.

Martin Welch

Its K.W.V.R. days over, No. 69023 took part in the short-lived experiment of running steam-hauled passenger trains over the private Derwent Valley Railway from York to Dunnington. Minus smokebox number, it waits patiently for passengers at York (Layerthorpe) on 14th May 1977. The Worth Valley connection is further strengthened by the presence of the N.E.R. inspection saloon.

John Sagar

Below: No. 69023 has now found a good home on the North Yorkshire Moors Railway and takes water at Grosmont on 29th April 1984 after a round trip to Pickering.

John Sagar

BRITISH RAILWAYS STANDARD CLASS '4MT' 4-6-0 No. 75078

Portrait of No. 75078. **John Sagar**

Below: Built at Swindon in 1956, No. 75078 was allocated to the Southern Region of British Railways for the whole of its main line career. It was withdrawn from service in 1966 when barely ten years old. For a lengthy period it worked from Basingstoke shed. In original single chimney form it awaits departure from Basingstoke shortly after entering service.

P. Jervis collection

Experiments revealed that the performance of these engines could be improved by front end modifications and the fitting of a double chimney. Twenty-two of the eighty locomotives in the class were eventually altered, among them No. 75078. This picture, taken at Eastleigh on 13th May 1962, also shows the engine fitted with a.w.s.   **P. Jervis collection**

Desperately in need of a clean, No. 75078 passes Bournemouth shed with a train for Bournemouth Central in August 1965. Note the Hawksworth-designed carriage behind the engine. A sister engine rests in the shed yard along with rebuilt 'West Country' 4-6-2 No. 34018 **Axminster**.

A.G. Storey

Right: The '4MT' 4-6-0s were a familiar sight on the Somerset and Dorset line in the years leading up to closure. They were drafted in to replace ageing '2P' 4-4-0s and frequently acted as pilot engines on heavy summer trains over the Mendips. Though not one of the Somerset and Dorset regulars, No. 75078 did occasionally work over the line while based at Bournemouth. On 1st October 1965 it could be seen leaving Chilcompton with a Templecombe-Bath train.

the late Derek Cross

Below: These modern 4-6-0s were eminently suitable for use on long distance passenger services with fairly light loads over secondary routes. Occasionally they aspired to greater things, as evinced by No. 75078 climbing out of Brockenhurst with the 15.35 Waterloo-Bournemouth of 23rd June 1966. The engine was withdrawn soon afterwards.

P. Hutchinson

No. 75078 was rescued from Barry scrapyard by the Standard '4' Locomotive Preservation Society and, after a five year restoration programme, entered Worth Valley service in early Spring 1977. A resurgent No. 75078 joins in the patriotic fervour of June that year.

J.R. Carter

19th March 1978 found No. 75078 at Ingrow, struggling for adhesion with the Railway's 30 ton capacity steam crane and tool van. The crane has since been sold to the Severn Valley Railway.

John Sagar

The fireman surfaces for air as No. 75078, carrying a west of England headcode, heads south west through Ingrow on a hot August day in 1978.
John Sagar

Opposite page: Evening shadows, Oakworth, July 1979.

John Sagar

Above: No. 75078 tries out the newly-commissioned water column at Keighley on 15th May 1983.

John Sagar

Left: Fireman's-eye view. **John Sagar**

BRITISH RAILWAYS STANDARD CLASS '2MT' 2-6-0 No. 78022

Right: These lightweight 2-6-0s, closely related to the small Moguls designed for the L.M.S. by H.G. Ivatt, were perfectly at ease on secondary passenger services. No. 78022 heads a Chinley-Sheffield (Midland) train in classic setting at Chinley North Junction.

Eric Oldham

Above: The sixty-five engines of this class were very much maids of all work and could also be seen on freight, shunting and station pilot duties. No. 78022 stands at Sheffield (Midland) in the early 1960s.

P. Jervis collection

Right centre: No. 78022 at Doncaster in late 1962. Ousted by diesels, it was soon to move to Lancashire, where it remained until withdrawn from Lostock Hall shed in September 1966.

G. Ibbetson

Bottom: The derelict No. 78022, as delivered from Barry scrapyard in June 1975. Good progress has since been made with this ambitious restoration project. Most missing parts have been obtained and a new tender tank fabricated. When it returns to service, No. 78022 should prove to be a very useful engine thanks to its many modern operating facilities.

John Sagar

Opposite page: No. 78022 spent the first eight years of its working life, from 1954 to 1962, at Sheffield (Millhouses) depot. In filthy condition, it keeps company with an unidentified 'Jubilee' class 4-6-0 at Leeds City on 13th May 1961, having just run down light from Holbeck shed.

Robin Lush

BRITISH RAILWAYS STANDARD CLASS '4MT' 2-6-4 SIDE TANK
No. 80002

No. 80002 stands at its birthplace, Derby, on 21st October 1952. These locomotives were designed and built under the supervision of R.A. Riddles and intended for short-distance freight and suburban passenger traffic. The recessed square panel below the cab windows was meant to accommodate tablet-catching apparatus on engines used in single line areas.

R.J. Buckley

A Scottish Region engine for the whole of its working life with B.R., No. 80002 rests in the shed yard at Polmadie, Glasgow on 27th June 1953. The shed staff kept No. 80002 and her sisters in immaculate condition. Note the power classification below the cab windows instead of in the normal position above the number. The cylinders were painted unlined black at this time.

A.G. Ellis

An atmospheric view of empty stock of Mount Florida football specials stabled in Muirhouse sidings, Glasgow on 14th April 1956.

W.A.C. Smith

No. 80002 at Greenock (Lynedoch) with the 15.30 Princes Pier — Glasgow St. Enoch, 23rd August 1958.

W.A.C. Smith

On the Glasgow Central Low Level line, No. 80002 arrives at Crow Road with the 17.19 Rutherglen-Possil of 9th September 1959.

W.A.C. Smith

Following transfer to Beattock shed, No. 80002 was used to bank heavy trains up the severe Beattock bank. In April 1963 it assists a 'Black Five' near Harthope with a Carlisle-Perth parcels train.

the late Derek Cross

Above: No. 80002 enjoys a brief respite from its banking duties as it leaves Beattock with a brake van for Moffat in the mid-1960s.

T.G. Hepburn/Rail Archive Stephenson

Right: In February 1967, No. 80002 rubs shoulders with two B.R. standard '4MT' 2-6-0s at Beattock depot. It was removed to Cowlairs for use as a stationary boiler soon afterwards.

N.R. Knight

No. 80002 relegated to the status of carriage warming boiler at Cowlairs sidings on 25th April 1967. Part of the bunker had been cut away to facilitate coaling. The engine survived in this state to become the last B.R. steam locomotive to perform any useful work in Scotland. The firebox problems which have bedevilled its Worth Valley career probably date from this period.

W.A.C. Smith

This handsome locomotive was towed to Keighley via Beattock and Ais Gill summits on 20th May 1969. After extensive mechanical and boiler work and a complete repaint it entered Worth Valley service on 22nd August 1971. An immaculate No. 80002 poses at Haworth on 10th July that year. A large B.R. emblem was applied because the smaller variety was unobtainable at the time.

Martin Welch

Guest of honour at the Society's Annual Dinner on 6th November 1971 was the late R.A. Riddles, designer of the B.R. standard locomotives. The following day he was able to sample his own work at Haworth.

Martin Welch

Above: Also on 7th November 1971, No. 80002 is assisted away from a very wet Haworth by D0226 as it hauls the newly-arrived **City of Wells** up to Oxenhope.

Martin Welch

Right: No. 80002 in sylvan setting by Bridgehouse Beck on 23rd April 1973 with the noon train from Keighley. The standard tank was withdrawn from traffic in September 1973 when the need for extensive and costly firebox repairs became evident. Following several setbacks it is now hoped that this powerful and popular locomotive will return to service in the not too distant future.

Nigel Hunt

BRITISH RAILWAYS STANDARD CLASS '9F' 2-10-0 No. 92220 'EVENING STAR'

Nameplate and plaque of No. 92220, the last steam locomotive built for British Railways.

John Sagar

After a spell of service at Cardiff Canton depot, No. 92220 was one of the '9F' 2-10-0s which revolutionised services on the Somerset and Dorset line in the 1960s. On 8th September 1962, **Evening Star** performed the melancholy duty of heading the last north-bound 'Pines Express' over the S. & D. With driver Peter Smith at the controls, No. 92220 thunders away from Blandford. The 12-coach train, weighing some 470 tons gross, was the heaviest authenticated load ever taken over Masbury summit without assistance.

Tony Richardson

A featherweight load for a '9F' as No. 92220 waits at Evercreech Junction station with the 13.10 'down' local from Bath, 12th September 1963.

Ivo Peters

Already starting to look neglected and run-down, **Evening Star** stands at Oxford shed in 1963 with one of its distant ancestors, a G.W.R. 2-8-0.

Richard S. Greenwood

Above: Ever since it emerged from Swindon in March 1960, No. 92220 has been a popular performer on enthusiasts' tours. On 20th September 1964 it takes a 'Farewell to Steam Tour' from London Victoria through Wimbledon. By now the '9F' was allocated to Cardiff (East Dock). It was withdrawn in early Spring 1965 following collision damage.

D.A. Buckett

Left: Evening Star was sent on loan to Haworth until a place was ready for it in the new National Railway Museum at York. The engine made its debut in Worth Valley passenger service on 21st July 1973. Its massive proportions are lit to perfection as it accelerates away from Damems loop in Summer 1973.

Martin Welch

Right: No. 92220 gave the Railway its first taste of operating a glamorous main line express engine. It also provided plenty of excuses for the use of cherished headboards from former times! Looking every bit as good as the real thing, No. 92220 blasts out of Ingrow tunnel on 22nd March 1975 with a Yorkshire version of the 'Pembroke Coast Express.'

Martin Welch

Bottom: Evening Star also introduced the Railway to the operation of main line steam specials. On 31st May 1975 it powered a Leeds-Grange-over-Sands excursion, organised jointly with the L.C.G.B. No. 92220 is seen making light work of its 14-coach train as it passes through the Yorkshire Dales.

Worthrail Photo Archive

The '9F' rouses the echoes near Oxenhope in the Summer of 1975. It left the Railway soon afterwards for the Stockton & Darlington Railway sesquicentenary celebrations and, ultimately, its new home in the N.R.M. at York. This historic locomotive was a great attraction at Haworth and the Society was privileged to be able to offer it a home for two years.

Martin Welch

Above: Evening Star in close-up.   **John Sagar**

Left: No. 92220 leads a very active retirement at York, taking a major role in the return to steam on B.R. main lines. A long way from Masbury, but still very much 'on song', the engine roars through Micklefield with one of the B.R. 'York Circular' trains, 2nd July 1978.

John Sagar

WORTH VALLEY RAILWAY

A Service of Remembrance for our
late President, the Rt. Rev. Eric Treacy
will be held at Haworth Station on
Saturday, 2nd September 1978
at 3.15 p.m.
[Speaker: The Very Revd. Brandon Jackson,
Provost of Bradford Cathedral]

All passenger fares taken on that day will be
donated to St. Christopher's Home, Derby
(former Railway Servants' Orphanage)
whose Patron is H.M. The Queen Mother.
To help this Charity you should please travel to
Haworth by Worth Valley trains.
(Depart Keighley 2.20 p.m. or 3.07 p.m. and
all usual trains as per timetable).

For use on that day we shall again have the
loan of the famous engine 'EVENING STAR'
which we also expect to have in use on
September 3rd, 17th & 24th. That engine then
leaves us on the 30th September for a main
line excursion also in memory of Eric Treacy.

Enquiries — Telephone Haworth 43629

Evening Star was one of the favourite locomotives of the Society's late President, Eric Treacy, Lord Bishop of Wakefield. A railway photographer of great renown, Eric died whilst photographing the engine at Appleby on 13th May 1978. To commemorate his work for the Railway and his influence in bringing No. 92220 to Haworth, a Service of Remembrance was arranged for 2nd September 1978 and No. 92220 most appropriately worked the special train. It is seen departing from Haworth at the end of the Service.

John Sagar

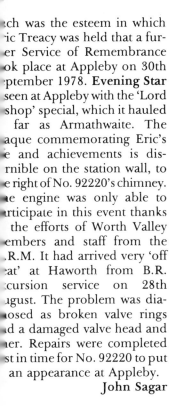

ch was the esteem in which ic Treacy was held that a fur er Service of Remembrance ok place at Appleby on 30th ptember 1978. **Evening Star** seen at Appleby with the 'Lord shop' special, which it hauled far as Armathwaite. The aque commemorating Eric's e and achievements is dis rnible on the station wall, to e right of No. 92220's chimney. e engine was only able to rticipate in this event thanks the efforts of Worth Valley embers and staff from the R.M. It had arrived very 'off at' at Haworth from B.R. cursion service on 28th ugust. The problem was dia osed as broken valve rings d a damaged valve head and er. Repairs were completed st in time for No. 92220 to put an appearance at Appleby.

John Sagar

HUDSWELL, CLARKE 0-4-0 SADDLE TANK 'LORD MAYOR'

Lord Mayor is the smallest steam locomotive on the Worth Valley Railway. It was built in 1893 and has led the varied sort of existence associated with contractors' locomotives.

Left: Perhaps the highlight of **Lord Mayor's** career was its use on the construction of the Castle Cary line for the G.W.R. Here, however, it is pictured engaged in quarrying work at an unspecified location about 1947.

Ben Wade collection

Bottom: Later in its travels, **Lord Mayor** works a short train in February 1957 over the Liverpool Overhead Railway in conjunction with demolition of that famous Merseyside institution.

Merseyside County Museums

Above: Tipping the scales at a mere 15½ tons in full working order, **Lord Mayor** sees only irregular use on the Worth Valley. It is normally resident at Ingrow and shunts the yard there on 29th May, 1983.

John Sagar

Right: Lord Mayor dons his raincoat, Keighley, 8th April 1984. Known as 'kettles' in Worth Valley parlance, these small locomotives have their own special charm.

John Sagar

CRANFORD IRONSTONE COMPANY MANNING, WARDLE 0-6-0 SADDLE TANK 'SIR BERKELEY'

Sir Berkeley is another small contractors' locomotive. It was built in Leeds in 1891 as an example of Manning, Wardle's standard 'L' class. Several hundred were built and engines of this type could be found at work all over the world. **Sir Berkeley** saw

widespread use on railway construction works – most notably the London extension of the Great Central Railway – before passing into the hands of the Cranford Ironstone Company in 1934.

Left: Siesta time for the driver of **Sir Berkeley** at Cranford in July 1953.

Frank Jones

Below: A somewhat unsightly cab was fitted to **Sir Berkeley** at Cranford in 1957 to give better protection to the driver. The engine also acquired a mechanical lubricator. It was able to haul four 20 ton loaded wagons up the stiff 1 in 30 gradients at the quarry.

J.P. Mullett

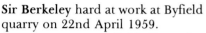

Sir Berkeley hard at work at Byfield
quarry on 22nd April 1959.

R.M. Casserley

In January 1965 **Sir Berkeley** became the second locomotive to arrive at Haworth under Preservation Society auspices. The cab was soon removed and replaced by the original brass-rimmed weatherboard which had been located at Cranford. Because of its undeniably vintage appearance, **Sir Berkeley** has caught the eye of film makers. During filming of the B.B.C. version of 'The Railway Children', it heads a short freight between Oakworth and Mytholmes on 26th March 1968. This delightful little engine has been out of use for several years, but plans are afoot to return it to steam before very long.

John S. Whiteley

HAYDOCK FOUNDRY 0-6-0 WELL TANK 'BELLEROPHON'

This is the Worth Valley's oldest locomotive, having been built in 1874 by Richard Evans & Co. Ltd. at Haydock Foundry for use on that firm's colliery lines in south Lancashire. Interesting mechanical features are the outside Gooch valve gear and the use of piston valves some years prior to their general adoption by main line or private builders. Following nationalisation of the coal industry in 1947, **Bellerophon** was taken into N.C.B. stock. It ended its working life at Lea Green Colliery near St. Helens as late as 1964. In view of its remarkable longevity and great historical importance, **Bellerophon** was eventually donated to the Society for preservation and came to Haworth in November 1966.

An early study of **Bellerophon**.   Terry Sykes collection

Top: **Bellerophon** in early N.C.B. days at Haydock. Note the cover over the slidebars and the Ramsbottom safety valves.

G. Alliez

Centre: **Bellerophon** at Haydock on 11th May 1957 following overhaul. 'J94' buffers and Ross Pop safety valves have been fitted and the slidebar cover has been discarded. The plate on the cab side denotes that the engine was permitted to work over certain B.R. lines.

A.C. Gilbert

Bottom: Looking very much like something left over from another age, **Bellerophon** shunts at Haydock on 12th October 1957.

J.F. Ward

For the past few years Worth Valley member Terry Sykes and a small band of helpers have been working to restore **Bellerophon** for occasional light use on the Railway. Grant aid from the Science Museum and the involvement of the Vintage Carriages Trust in the project have considerably hastened the work. The magnitude of the task is illustrated by this shot of Terry surveying his kit of parts following the fitting of a new smokebox to the boiler.

Terry Sykes collection

Bellerophon in winter.   John Davies

BIRDS OF PASSAGE

The connection with B.R. at Keighley makes for easy transfer of locomotives and rolling stock. Over the years the Railway has received several distinguished visitors. It is very much hoped that, where axle-loadings and clearances permit, this will be a feature of Worth Valley practice for a long time to come.

Gresley 'K4' 2-6-0 No. 3442 **The Great Marquess** at Keighley platform 3 with 'The Mercian' rail tour of 16th April 1967.

Howard Malham

Flying Scotsman visited Keighley in February 1980 to appear in a t.v. commercial. It even ventured up to Haworth after dark for servicing. No. 4472 rests between 'takes' at platform 4.

John Sagar

Left: Two famous Southern express engines renew acquaintance at Keighley, 15th November 1980. No. 850 had worked down from Carlisle earlier that day and, after turning at Shipley called in at Keighley to take water. It then towed **City of Wells** to Steamtown, Carnforth for repairs which would bring it up to main line operating condition.

John Sagar

Below: The Summer of 1981 saw a very unusual visitor in the shape of **Lion**, the 1838-built Liverpool & Manchester Railway 0-4-2 tender engine. During its stay it was permitted to work a limited number of trips over the branch with its replica carriages. On 14th September 1981 it stands at Oxenhope during a filming assignment. **Lion**, of course, gained great celebrity from its starring role in 'The Titfield Thunderbolt'.

John Sagar

Above: The North Eastern Loco-motive Preservation Group's Peppercorn 'K1' class 2-6-0 No. 2005 spent three weeks on the Railway in March 1982. On the 7th of that month it makes an energetic departure from Keighley with a special train for original members of the K.W.V.R.P.S.

Brian Dobbs

Right: The 'K1' gallops up to Oakworth with a van train on 28th March 1982.

D.J. Fowler

Rapidly becoming an established part of the Worth Valley scene is this Somerset & Dorset Joint Railway '7F' 2-8-0 No. 13809. It has visited the branch in both 1983 and 1984 whilst in the north of England on rail tour duty. Freshly-arrived from the Midland Railway Centre, Butterley, it takes a wagon bearing scaffolding and the G.W.R. 'Toad' brake van out of Oakworth yard on 6th April 1984.

John Sagar

No. 13809 drifts into Ingrow on 8th April 1984. This engine has won many friends on the Worth Valley and further visits are eagerly awaited!

John Sagar

154

Hudswell, Clarke 0-6-0T No. 32 **Gothenburg** explodes out of Keighley at dusk on 8th April 1984. This is a sister engine to No. 31 **Hamburg** and is normally kept at the Bury depot of the East Lancashire Railway Preservation Society. It had been transferred temporarily to the Worth Valley for running trials.

John Sagar

Men of Steam

Oxenhope, 1960. **The late
W. Hubert Foster**

Dressed for the part. **John
Sagar**

Dick Hardy (former Shed-
master, Stewarts Lane) and
friend. **John Sagar**

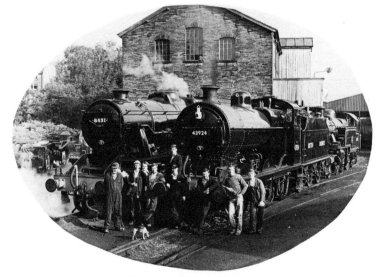

Teamwork. **John Sagar**

WORTH VALLEY LAMENT

Although the Worth Valley has a magnificent collection of locomotives, it is perhaps a matter for regret that not all those classes which once worked regularly over the line are represented. Illustrated on this and the next page are three types which the Railway would dearly love still to have at its disposal.

Above: Midland Railway 0-4-4T No. 58040 leaves Oakworth shortly after nationalisation. The loop was still in use.

N.E. Stead

Left: Sparse patronage for Ivatt '4MT' 2-6-0 No. 43114 at Oxenhope in the late 1950s.

collection of the late
W. Hubert Foster

Midland '3F' 0-6-0 No. 43586 at Oakworth with the Society special of
23rd June 1962. This was the last B.R. passenger train to Oxenhope.
Richard S. Greenwood

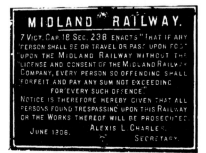

MIDLAND RAILWAY.
7 VICT. CAP. 18 SEC. 238 ENACTS "THAT IF ANY
PERSON SHALL BE OR TRAVEL OR PASS UPON FOOT
UPON THE MIDLAND RAILWAY WITHOUT THE
LICENSE AND CONSENT OF THE MIDLAND RAILWAY
COMPANY, EVERY PERSON SO OFFENDING SHALL
FORFEIT AND PAY ANY SUM NOT EXCEEDING
FOR EVERY SUCH OFFENCE."
NOTICE IS THEREFORE HEREBY GIVEN THAT ALL
PERSONS FOUND TRESPASSING UPON THIS RAILWAY
OR THE WORKS THEREOF WILL BE PROSECUTED.
JUNE 1906.   ALEXIS L. CHARLES,
                    SECRETARY.

FINALE

Here's to the next twenty years!   John Sagar

If you are interested in helping to keep steam alive in the Worth Valley, please write to:

Keighley & Worth Valley Railway Preservation Society

Haworth Station,
Haworth,
Keighley,
Yorkshire.

Typeset by:
Alphaset, 356 Portswood Road, Portswood, Southampton SO2 3SB

Printed by:
Netherwood Dalton & Co., Bradley Mills, Huddersfield, Yorks.